Early Responses

Mystics have always faced a choi[ce...]
the housetops' and keeping silent [...]
cule and contempt, while silence [...]
very source of their spiritual inspiration. Emmanuel Elliott has
made his choice. The result is a compelling first-hand story of a
pilgrim's progress, all too real and yet evoking aspects of *The Da
Vinci Code*.

Alexis Léonas, PhD
Biblical Scholar and author of L'Aube des Traducteurs' *Paris, Cerf, 2007*

THE DAWNING will take you on an extraordinary journey
with a man as he seeks enlightenment and a greater understanding of spiritual truth. Come, join Emmanuel on this truly
fascinating story, for you too will discover the spiritual wisdom
as his experiences impact your life as they did his.

Nick Bunick
Author of the best-selling 'The Messengers'

There are many kinds of adventure stories that are published
every year. My favourites are generally stories of spiritual
adventure – stories of how one's life has been shifted and
moved by psycho-spiritual factors. Emmanuel has written such
a book: a real life spiritual adventure story that reveals the
amazing possibilities of change within each of us.

Hal Stone, PhD
Co-author of 'Embracing Our Selves' (etc., etc.)
and co-creator of Voice Dialogue International

This is a truly extraordinary book. It contains a message that
could change the world. I read it with a mixture of fascination,
discomfort – and hope.
An account of a lifelong search for spiritual truth, it is also
something of a detective story, one in which intriguing
questions are posed – and answered.
Read this book with an open mind. You may be surprised
where it takes you.

The Book Review Service (U.K.)

Emmanuel gives a clear accounting of a remarkable life journey, one that reveals a profound spiritual path full of great insights and integrity. It is easy and fun to read.
Dr. Judith Kravitz
Author of Breathe Deep, Laugh Loudly
and Founder of the Transformational Breath Foundation

The Dawning tells of a new spiritual opening, to which more than a dozen other books already bear witness.
What Emmanuel Elliott has done is to go one step farther and connect this awakening of the soul with the prophecy made at Fatima, Portugal, in 1917. Has the Second Coming already happened like 'a thief in the night' as foretold in the Bible? Is this the reason the Third Secret of Fatima, intended to be revealed to the world in 1960, was suppressed?
The ramifications of this book can barely be contemplated. The great religions of the world should surely be united in the one supreme aim of Surrender to the Will of God. This is already the ostensible aim of both Christianity and Islam, but it has got snared and enmeshed in man's thinking, producing divisions and dogma. Is a great reconciliation now about to happen?
Anthony Bright-Paul
Author of My Stairway to Subud

THE DAWNING
A Grace Untold

The Third Secret of Fatima and the Coming of Subud

Emmanuel Elliott

DAWN CHORUS
PUBLISHING

Gloucester, England

THE DAWNING
by Emmanuel Elliott
First Edition

Copyright © 2009 by Emmanuel Elliott

The word Subud is a registered mark of the World Subud Association. All extracts from the talks of Bapak Mhd Subuh Sumohadiwidjojo are the copyright of the World Subud Association.

All rights reserved. No part of this book may be reproduced or transmitted by any means without permission from the author, except for the inclusion of brief quotations in a review.

The right of Emmanuel Elliott to be identified as the author of this work has been asserted by him in accordance with the Copyright, Designs and Patents Act 1988.

British Library Cataloguing in Publication Data.
A catalogue record for this book is available from the British Library.

Printed in the United Kingdom
ISBN: 978-0-9562878-0-9

Cover and book design by Marianna Unson Price.
Email: annaprice@skydsl.com.ph.

Published by

P.O. Box 2184
Gloucester, GL3 9AU
dawncp@blueyonder.co.uk

*This book is dedicated
to the memory of*

*Bapak
Muhammad Subuh Sumohadiwidjojo*

and of

Mark and Istimah Week

Whosoever will lose his life for my sake
shall find it.
Matthew 16:25

It is important to die the special death
before the common death.
Shaikh 'Abd al-Qadir al-Jilani

To surrender identification with that
which was presumed to be 'me' allows
the real Me to shine forth as the immanent quality
of Divinity that is the source
of the unencumbered reality of 'I.'
Dr. David R. Hawkins, MD, PhD

Acknowledgements

*I am extremely grateful for the care and
commitment of two fine editors
- Susannah Ortego and Ilaina Lennard -
whose invaluable and timely contributions
were separated by nearly twenty years.*

*I must also record my appreciation to
Raymond van Sommers, Sandra Week,
Simón Cherpitel and Maria Elliott
for their moral support and practical help;*

*and to Andrew Bromley, John Kirby,
Amanda Farmer, Maggie Pugh,
Marcus Bolt, Leonard Hurd
and Michael Menduno
for their constructive feedback
along the way.*

*My special thanks to reviewer
Harris Smart;*

*and to my designer
- Marianna Unson Price -
whose expertise was equalled
only by her infinite patience.*

"It has become known
that something will arise in the East
and that from here it will spread."

Bapak

"It was not enough to
have experienced this for myself.
I knew that I had to have the
courage to bear witness to it."

Emmanuel Elliott

And it shall come to pass after this,
that I will pour out my spirit upon all flesh;
and your sons and your daughters shall prophesy,
your old men shall dream dreams,
your young men shall see visions.
Joel 2:28

Much of what you read in this book may
challenge your credulity.
Its pages are spilling over with 'prophesy,'
with 'the dreaming of dreams,'
and with the 'seeing of visions.'
Can such things really have happened now,
in the late twentieth century and the early twenty-first?

It is one thing to take in our stride the supernatural events
recorded in the holy books of whatever religion
we may subscribe to and in the annals of bygone eras.
It is quite another to accept that the miraculous can become
the stuff of everyday life for a very ordinary person
from the humblest of backgrounds in this materialistic age
of hype and celebrity culture.

Nevertheless, this is what I am asking you to believe.

And I swear
– by all that I hold most dear, by all that is most holy –
that every word of it is true.

Contents

1

"Hold Everything!"

London, England, 1957. Winter was fast approaching, as was my twenty-first birthday, and I was a sergeant in the Royal Air Force, a member of the personal staff of the Commander-in-Chief, Fighter Command. My immediate boss was Squadron Leader (later Air Commodore) Roy H. Crompton. Quite apart from our normal working relationship, Roy and I had for some time shared common ground of a less official nature: the search for Truth. We were in the habit of comparing notes on the latest mystical literature we came across, discussion groups we attended, and so on. This sharing was of great value to us both.

My own quest had begun in earnest around the age of sixteen. Being expected to go to church several times each Sunday while other kids in the neighbourhood ran free had resulted in an adverse reaction in my early teens to what I saw as an overly rigid Christian upbringing. Nevertheless, an orientation toward the Divine had been well and truly established within me, although I struggled with the idea that any one religion could lay sole claim to spiritual reality when generations of sincere people were born into such a diversity of religious and cultural environments. Surely the answer had to be much deeper than the dogmatic, superficial exclusivity of one group or another. Was it not possible that all the great religions, all true ways to spiritual

1

knowledge, had sprung from the same pure source to which they were all aspiring to return?

An early breakthrough was my discovery in the public library of a slim volume on Buddhism by Christmas Humphries. I was about sixteen years old and can still remember the excitement with which I devoured this little book. It seemed to throw open a great window in my mind: here was the unmistakable ring of truth from a tradition totally alien to the one that had been inculcated within me during childhood. After visiting a Buddhist monastery in London, I went on to read a great many other books on Buddhism, as well as the writings of Sufi, Jewish and Hindu mystics. The works of Krishnamurti, Rudolf Steiner, Gurdjieff and Ouspensky also played a part in broadening my perception. The most memorable impression of all from that period was the story of Ramakrishna. This nineteenth century Indian saint was moved to devote three months respectively to the practice of each of the major world religions in turn. At the end of this experiment he was able to bear witness that in essence they were all the same; that each led to the same inner bliss.

My friend was pursuing his own lines of enquiry of course, and it was not unusual, when time allowed, for us to interrupt the working day with an exchange of ideas. What was unusual, however, was the light in Roy's eyes one morning when he bounced into the office and said, "Hold everything!" It seemed that he had had a telephone call the previous evening from an old friend, author and journalist Derek Dempster, telling him that he had just heard from Michael Scott,[1] himself an earnest seeker living in Tangier. Michael wanted him to know about a visit to England by a Javanese master called Pak Subuh. According to Michael, this man was able to put people in touch with the power of God within themselves. He had been staying at the Gurdjieff Institute at Coombe Springs near Richmond, which was run by John G. Bennett.

It transpired that Pak Subuh – usually referred to as Bapak - had indeed spent several weeks in Surrey as the guest of John Bennett, a leading figure in the movement dedicated to the Gurdjieff method of working upon the self. It seemed that this man from Indonesia had set in motion something of a spiritual whirlwind by introducing Bennett and hundreds of his followers to a new spiritual way, a uniquely personal inner awakening.

There was something compelling about this report, and within days Roy and I were among a crowd gathered at Coombe Springs to hear Mr. Bennett talk about something called Subud. Subud, it seemed was the name of the movement now gaining ground in the West in the wake of Bapak's recent first visit to the hemisphere. The word Subud, Bennett told us, was a contraction of three Sanskrit words, meaning 'right living from

---

[1] Although Michael Scott, no matter how unwittingly, played a pivotal role in my hearing about Subud, we were not to meet for another thirty-three years. My first book, *Revelation Subud*, happened to find its way into his hands in 1992 just as he was about to spend a few days in retreat at the Ste. Wandrille Monastery in northern France – the same monastery, incidentally, where in 1959 John Bennett had 'opened' some of the monks and received the important revelation documented in a later chapter of this book. Upon his return to England, Michael contacted me and then joined me at my house in Hertfordshire for latihan. The next day, he phoned from a London hospital to say he'd been knocked down by a motor cycle: blinded in one eye during the war, he had been literally 'blind-sided' by the bike. At first, it was thought he had got away with multiple scrapes and bruises, but after a few days his doctor woke up to the fact that he also had a broken neck! Michael died ten days later, and I visited him on every one of those days, grateful to this day that I had such an opportunity to repay my immense debt of gratitude to the man who was responsible for my coming into contact with the latihan.

within according to the will of God.'[1]

My first impression of Mr. Bennett, or Mr. B as he was known to his students, was of a huge man, broad and 6' 3" tall, who radiated an aura of controlled energy, high intelligence and a palpable sensitivity.

Bennett told us something of the early life of Bapak himself and how he had received the powerful spiritual vibration now causing so much interest and excitement in this quiet corner of Surrey. The word Bapak, he told us, simply meant father or respected older man in Indonesian. Bapak's full name was Muhammad Subuh Sumohadiwidjojo.

"The transmission of this inner contact from one person to another is called the opening," Bennett explained. "After being opened you will be able to experience a spontaneous and ongoing spiritual exercise called the *latihan kejiwaan.*" (Hereinafter referred to as 'the latihan.')

As he spoke, I felt touched and calmed inside. I somehow knew that this was 'it,' and all my questioning fell away. A week later, returning in company with a railway carriage half full of other enquirers, I found it hard to understand why the others seemed to need to debate and analyse what Subud was all about. Although characteristically I would normally have been active in such a discussion, now somehow it was enough for me to sit quietly in tune with the inner certainty that possessed me.

As proof of our sincerity, and to give us time to find out all we could about Subud and the latihan, we were required to wait three months before being opened. It was a period that passed all too slowly for me. But pass it did, and on January 18, 1958, I

---

[1] If at any point during this narrative you would like further clarification about Subud and the latihan, about how Bapak himself first received the contact and about the process of purification that is inseparable from it, please go to Appendix B – What is Subud?

made my way back down to Coombe Springs from North London for the big event. My feelings were a mixture of nervousness and keen anticipation.

I was shown into a small upstairs room in the spacious country house that was Coombe Springs. There was nothing special about the room, no religious pictures or statues of any kind, no altar, no sense of the formal. It was just a simple sitting room with the furniture pushed back against the walls to create as much clear space as possible. It was late afternoon and a window looked out on a broad stretch of sunlit lawn. The room was already occupied by three or four other men, all in shirt sleeves, and I was asked to remove my jacket, shoes and tie. We were joined by a young Indonesian named Sjafrudin (pronounced Shafrudin), who slipped quietly and unobtrusively into the room at the last minute. Although I would get to know him later, back then I had no idea that Shaf was Bapak's key helper in the West at that time, having been left behind after Bapak's return to Indonesia.

There was no ceremony as such. All that happened was that one of the men read a short statement stating that they were there as witnesses to my wish to worship God. He went on to explain that it was only necessary for me to relax without concentrating my thinking and to freely follow whatever might arise with me. Then he said, "Begin."

I remember feeling tense, rather self-conscious, as the others began to move slowly around the room, some of them singing in a gentle, highly individual way. I also felt impatient to join in, but, to my surprise and slight irritation, my knees kept threatening to give way. Again and again, I forced myself to straighten up so as to be ready to begin my own spiritual exercise. Eventually it occurred to me that perhaps my body knew, better than my mind, that my latihan was trying to begin, and I decided to let it have its own way. Immediately and unexpectedly I fell to my knees in a spontaneous attitude of worship and surrender. With my body moving entirely of its own accord, my forehead touched the floor in total prostration whilst within my being I became aware of an energy flow, a sense of awe, that was quite new to me. A few minutes later, one of the men said, "Finish," and to my astonishment I realised that half an hour had passed.

Roy Crompton had received the contact the week before and had very kindly accompanied me to Coombe for my own opening. Now, one of the men, Pierre Elliott (no relation), escorted me back downstairs and handed me over to Roy. I felt very calm and at peace, very alive, and I noticed Pierre nod in response to Roy's enquiring glance. Yes, I had been 'opened.'

My life was never to be the same again. Although I had no way of knowing it, I had embarked upon a journey that would lead me through a series of truly extraordinary experiences, a path that would eventually penetrate to the very core of the Secret of Fatima[1] and lift the veil on the true nature of the Second Coming of Christ.

---

[1] During a series of apparitions at Fatima, Portugal, in 1917, the Virgin Mary revealed four 'secrets' to three simple village children. Three of these were made known to the world in 1927; one of them was withheld.

2

A Spiritual Apprenticeship

I had been opened exactly one month after getting married. Suzanna and I had got to know each other a couple of years earlier as pen friends while she was a nurse in England and I was based at the NATO headquarters of Allied Air Forces Central Europe at Fontainebleau, about sixty kilometers from Paris.

Born in India, the daughter of an Army major, Susanna spent her formative years in Bangalore and later Singapore, coming to live in England when she was 12 years old.

It was abundantly clear to me from our first meeting that Suzanna was pure gold: an attractive, brave and delightful girl whose personal qualities resulted in her being made head girl of her school in Truro, Cornwall. One incident from our early years together sums up her character perfectly. We were enjoying a lazy afternoon on the beach at Dawlish Warren in Devon one summer, soaking up the sun and idly watching the swimmers. One young boy in particular had caught our attention: riding a surfboard, he had paddled out into deep water where quite suddenly he seemed to fall off the board and disappear from sight. Alarmingly, he failed to surface, but somehow – perhaps because I had played a similar trick myself as a boy with an old cavalry sabre thrust into the ground beside my apparently lifeless body! – I just *knew* that this little drama was being played out for the benefit of the watchers on the beach. But Suzanna didn't hesitate. She leapt to her feet and had raced the hundred yards or so to the water's edge before the boy's head reappeared alongside his surfboard. Although she was by no means a strong swimmer, I have not the slightest doubt that she would have done her utmost to reach the boy and bring him safely ashore.

A well-grounded, well-rounded personality, Suzanna had never been a spiritual seeker. Nevertheless, she was soon influenced by my enthusiasm for the latihan and three months later she too came to Subud. Before long, both my parents followed suit, and it was lovely from time to time to be able to do latihan with Dad.

◆ ◆ ◆

Coombe Springs in the late 1950s had to be the spiritual hub of the universe, or so it seemed: an instant Mecca miraculously transported to one of the greenest and most pleasant parts of England's green and pleasant land. Every night, scores of eager new Subud members of all ages, from every walk of life and from far and wide made their way to this sprawling country house and its seven acres of lawn and garden to take their places in the round of latihan*s* that kept the place throbbing late into the evening. There would be latihans every half hour through-out each evening, thirty people at a time, and it was necessary to get there as early as possible to add your name to the earliest possible grouping. While we waited to take our turn, we would gather in the impromptu coffee shop set up to cater to the ex-cited throng. It was without doubt a very special time, a very special atmosphere. A great event was under way, one that would surely encompass the whole world in no time at all.

My own twice weekly visits from North London – by way of bus, underground train, coach and a mile walk at the end of the trek – were easily the high spots of a life made suddenly rich and meaningful. In finding the latihan I knew that I had come home. I was discovering that the Kingdom of Heaven really was within me. Gone was the earnest scanning of library shelves and the mental harvesting of theories and philosophies. I knew that I had been blessed beyond measure: that the *reality* of the latihan was what I had been searching for all along.

Every latihan was an adventure, a magical mystery tour of sound and movement, as this miraculous inner contact spread its wings and led me, often quite literally, on a merry dance of self-discovery. Simultaneously both relaxing and exhilarating, each latihan was, superficially, a welcome release from the tensions and pressure of the moment. More deeply, I sensed that I was participating in one of the marvels of the age, an awesome dispensation of grace and revelation comparable to any in history.

The latihan, it was becoming increasingly clear, was a spiritual bonanza in which, through the power of God alone, we were gradually being brought to the feet of the Most High in the purest form of worship imaginable.

◆ ◆ ◆

By now I was stationed at Fighter Command HQ in Hertfordshire, and within a few months local groups began to form wherever there were enough people in a neighbourhood to make it possible. I was the youngest among the dozen or so founding members of the Northwood (Middlesex) group, initially meeting in the home of Gordon and Joan Creighton in Rickmansworth. This was later to develop into the Loudwater group, still active today at Loudwater Farm, Rickmansworth, Herts.

The comparatively rapid early spread of the latihan and the proliferation of small groups in the U.K. at that time created a pressing need for local helpers to look after new members, and

I was one of many youthful and inexperienced people pressed into service to meet the emergency. For a 21 year old with just a few months of latihan under his belt, this was laughably premature.

After I had blithely followed the spiritual exercise for a couple of years, a period which in retrospect could perhaps be described as something of a spiritual honeymoon, its action began to work more deeply, cutting through the superficial structure of my ego. I began to be painfully aware of some of the less savoury aspects of my nature: timidity, lust, jealousy and impatience being prominent among them. I was horrified at this pricking of the bubble of my self-image. It was not until years later that I came across the Bapak quotation that was to become my lifelong creed: "Man is required only to surrender, to surrender with *acceptance* and a willingness to let go." Upon this attitude, I was to discover, 'hangs all the law and the prophets' of the spiritual life.

I feel in fact that this advice may well have been what Jesus had in mind when he said, "Take up your cross and follow me." Back then, however, instead of accepting the experience as a necessary insight into my own nature arising out of the process of inner separation and purification that had been set in motion, this growing awareness engendered a sense of shame and self-reproach. I was particularly troubled by the insecure aspects of my character. I found myself undergoing a period of emotional disturbance, one in which I experienced incomprehensible states of general anxiety and intense fear. For two whole weeks during this phase, both day and night, I *knew* that I was about to die! I had no idea what was happening, but it was terrifying.

In my confusion, I wrote to Bapak for clarification and Sudarto, one of the longest-serving Indonesian helpers, replied that their testing and receiving indicated that something had happened to me as a child to make me afraid of death. I was experiencing such terror now, he told me, because the latihan had begun to expose the injured aspects of my heart to the healing light.

His words evoked a vivid memory of how, as a child of about five years old during World War II, living immediately adjacent to an army barracks in Shakespeare Road, Exeter, our neighbourhood had been devastated in a bombing raid. I was carried to safety by a fireman, and to this day I can still see the blue floral patterned quilt in which I had been wrapped, our faces aglow with the flames of nearby burning buildings against a backdrop of searchlights probing the night sky. A stick of bombs had fallen within fifty yards of our house, killing and injuring neighbours, one of whom, an air raid warden, died just as he was ringing the bell of a house a few doors away to warn the inhabitants that a light was showing through their blackout curtains. The noise of the explosions was horrendous. For some years after the war, the bomb site created in just a few minutes that night served as a playground paradise for us kids, but during the raid and for hours afterwards it was hell on earth. Mum, Dad and I had taken refuge in the steel Anderson shelter erected in our small living room so that we were protected from the falling ceiling, the shower of broken glass and other debris from the blast. Witnessing my parent's vain attempts to hide their own fear, my fragile little world of trust and security also collapsed within me. "Please, can I go to Heaven now?" I asked my mother. I can't remember what she said in reply.

But there was nothing to worry about, Sudarto reassured me. "Your inner self is powerful enough to subdue your fears. It is only necessary to surrender everything to the power of God. Trust in God, and all anxiety will disappear from your heart."

There was also a message from Bapak: "Sometimes God allows those with a strong heart to experience the crisis state so as to enable them to know the true situation."

It was to be many years before I felt that I really understood what Bapak meant by this, but not long afterwards I felt that the ailing characteristics of my 'strong heart' were shown to me in a dream in which I was obliged to share a room with an old man, the embodiment of sorrow and self-pity, blindly blundering in all directions. He was immensely powerful, with muscles of iron, and no amount of struggle on my part could evict him. I came to feel that 'knowing the true situation' – in part at least – included accepting the need to recognize and differentiate between the false identity and patterns created by the conditioning of my heart and mind and the inner feeling of the true self gradually being separated from them. I saw that I could not disown or get rid of the strong old man, at that time such an entrenched aspect of my make-up. Instead, through awareness, I must learn to live with him, to be at peace with him, without allowing him to run my life in his blind and blundering way.

I was twenty-four years old, still in the R.A.F., and by now a member of the intelligence staff at the British Embassy in Washington, D.C., liaising with the Pentagon. I had come to hate Service life and was becoming increasingly dissatisfied and frustrated with what I saw as my meaningless role in the cold war machine. I had six years still to serve with the R.A.F. but longed to be free to pursue activities more in keeping with my true nature. Back at Coombe Springs, John Bennett had invited me to be his secretary, but because of my Service commitment I'd had to decline. At the time, he had received that I would be free of the R.A.F. by the time I was 25. Little did I know it, but his unlikely prediction was about to be fulfilled.

One day in the office, quite out of the blue, I was suddenly overwhelmed by the futility of my work. To my horror, I buried my face in my hands in full view of my colleagues and burst into tears. There had been no particular provocation or build-up of tension that I was aware of; it was as if a mask had been gently removed, to reveal the true feelings underneath. It was a strange and distinctly uncomfortable experience. Concerned at what might be construed as a threat to the highly sensitive material I handled, the authorities arranged for my immediate return to England. Within a month I was a civilian.

Before we left the United States, Mary Hyde, a much loved older member of the D.C. Subud group, received a message for me in the form of a rhyming couplet:

Reaction, Rhythm, Restoration;
Three Rs for Realization.

The Realization, she received, was connected with a bright light from far out in space, although it would be nearly thirty years before her words made sense.

♦ ♦ ♦

Suzanna's reaction to these events says a great deal about her character and inner strength. Although by now we had two small children, and despite the fact that she was really enjoying her life in America, my wife accepted the upheaval calmly and without complaint. Her support for me in my time of need was absolute.

As for me, alarmed at what had happened and dismayed at my seemingly infinite array of character defects, I began to develop a very ambivalent attitude to the latihan. This persisted for the next two years. I was just too involved to be able to recognize its purifying action at work, causing long-buried problem areas to rise to the surface. Instead of relaxing into the process and trusting God, therefore, I started to become afraid of the latihan. I blamed it for my own inner discord. I took my hand from the plough, in other words, and looked back.

My situation at that time was illustrated in what turned out to be a very precognitive dream – one of the first of what I later took to calling 'clear dreams.' In the dream I was climbing a very steep hill and, although the way ahead was smooth and not really difficult to climb, the summit was a long way off. I had only ascended about one tenth of the way when I looked down. At once my head swam and I lost my balance, whereupon a voice said, "Imagine falling from the *top!*" I knew that 'the top' signified the completion of a key stage of my process of purification and spiritual development, and that an attitude of trust and surrender would always be necessary along the way. Later in my journey I was to be glad of this early lesson. Like St. Peter who, however metaphorically, sank beneath the waves when he temporarily lost faith in his capacity to walk on water, I had learned the hard way that it would be vital to keep to the path I had chosen.

3

Inner Guidance

So many and varied are the ways in which Subud people receive inner guidance and personal revelation, that these fruits of the latihan can, I feel, be seen as having been foreshadowed in Joel 2:28: "And it shall come to pass after this, that I will pour out my spirit upon all flesh; and your sons and your daughters shall prophesy, your old men shall dream dreams, your young men shall see visions."

There are of course many other Biblical references to the spiritual significance of inspired dreams. And the Prophet Muhammad, the founder of Islam, spoke of the inward signs he received at the beginning of his mission as "true visions"[1] that came to him in his sleep. Bapak too, in Tokyo in 1967 – having earlier cautioned us that many dreams are only a projection of a person's ideas and imagination, and that clear receiving dreams are rarely experienced by people whose hearts and minds are still full of thoughts and emotions – said that sometimes "people have a dream which in its nature is an indication of what is going to happen. It then turns out that what they have received in their dream really comes true."

---

[1] Muhammad ibn Isma'il al–Bukhari 1,3

Throughout much of my more than fifty years of following the latihan, it has been quite commonplace to receive invaluable counsel in the form of dreams; to be shown in dreams the reality of my own state and that of other people and situations; and to dream of future events either just before or sometimes long before they occur. In fact I have been blessed with so much convincing personal experience of inner guidance manifesting through dreams that I have come to take the phenomenon somewhat for granted.

Much later in my latihan experience, guidance began to manifest itself in the form of visions, whereas from relatively early on such indications arose in the form of insight or intuitive knowledge, or as a spontaneous awareness of another's state. A typical, albeit uncomfortable, instance of the latter occurred when I opened a colleague's door and stepped into his office and almost doubled over with a sudden, sharp pain in my abdomen. "That's funny" he said, "I've been having excruciating stomach pains all afternoon."

This developing sensitivity also extended to picking up influences from lying in a bed that was not my own. One of the most graphic examples of this happened when I stayed with friends in Portland, Oregon. I was given a bed in a basement bedroom and the second my head touched the pillow I found myself straining at the head of a pack of runners exerting every nerve and sinew to reach the finish line. The next morning, when I mentioned this odd experience to my hostess, she was astonished. "That was our son's room," she explained, "and for his last three months before going to university he was totally committed to breaking the mile record at school before leaving. Nothing was more important to him."

The function of this inner antenna is not always so seemingly pointless. On one occasion I was driving a car crowded with our young family when I suddenly realised that just ahead was a snarl-up caused by an ambulance that had been forced to halt right across our path. I had been driving too fast and not paying full attention. It was too late to brake safely and I could see no way through. A serious accident seemed inevitable, and my mind went blank. In that instant the latihan took over my whole being. I watched in amazement while my hands and feet came alive and juggled with steering wheel, brake and gear change. I was astonished as, with unerring judgement and an extraordinary delicacy of touch, I piloted our hurtling vehicle through an unexpected gap in the traffic with inches to spare between us and the gaping faces to our left. Except that 'I' had nothing to do with it! Years later I asked my eldest daughter if she remembered the incident. "How could I ever forget it?" she laughed. "I couldn't believe it when you just took your hands off the wheel!"

Examples of such interaction between the miraculous and the mundane are legion among Subud members, one of my favourites being the story of a train passenger who was suddenly impelled for no discernible reason to vacate her seat and move to the one behind her. Seconds later a rock crashed through the window exactly where she had previously been sitting. Although showered with splinters of glass, she was completely unharmed.

Receiving by way of an inner voice also seems to be an increasingly common source of guidance for many people as they become more deeply established in the latihan. This phenomenon has been a natural and integral part of my own life for so long that it is perhaps appropriate at this point to recount the striking circumstances in which my own inner voice first made itself heard.

It was in the late 60s and I was in my early thirties and working as a herdsman on a dairy farm, something of a sabbatical from my usual more commercial pursuits. I looked after a Guernsey herd of about sixty milkers, and each day began with the chore of putting my charges through a 4 x 4 herringbone milking parlour. Such a milking shed accommodates an equal number of cows, in this case four, on each side of the herdsman, who works from a central well between them. This arrangement puts his head at the level of the upper part of the cow's legs and so allows him easy access to her udder.

Many herds have a percentage of troublemakers, who are of course well known to the herdsman. Towards these he will be especially cautious in view of his extreme vulnerability in the well of the parlour. In this particular herd, however, there were few such problem cases, and certainly never amongst the first thirty or so animals. These would make their way eagerly into the parlour in almost the same order every day, relaxed and looking forward to a good feed.

Dignity V was typical of this easygoing category. On the day in question she was, as usual, in the first group to enter the parlour, second only to Rosina, the acknowledged leader of the herd.

All seemed normal, and I fed the first four cows prior to washing their udders, a far from delicate procedure if one was to remove the dirt and mud picked up from a night in the field. It was also the sort of task one tended to carry out on automatic pilot and, having attended to Rosina, I reached out casually towards Dignity.

My hand was within a few inches of her udder when a great voice echoed through the parlour, seemingly both within and outside of me: "Be careful of this one." Strangely, I didn't think to question the fact of the voice itself. All that registered was its strong, commanding quality.

I froze and took a hard look at Dignity. Seeing nothing wrong, I flattened myself against cow number three and, using her body as a shield, reached out and very gently touched one of Dignity's teats. She responded instantly with the most ferocious kick imaginable, cleaving the air in deadly fashion precisely where my head would have been, but for that warning voice.

Subsequent examination revealed a horrible wound to the far side of the teat I had touched, an injury completely invisible from my position in the well of the parlour, and in a place that in the normal course of events I would have grasped with some vigour.

As it was, her response, even to the gentlest of touches, was such that I would never have survived that kick. It would have taken my head off.

Subud is the name of our Association. It is not the name of a spiritual knowledge. This spiritual knowledge has no name. Because we receive it directly from God, there is no name for it.

Bapak
Santiago De Chile, May 1967
(67 SCL 1)

4

Outer Endeavour

The farming diversion was but a brief interlude in a working life spent for the most part in a succession of business enterprises, always in a sales and marketing capacity. My abrupt departure from the R.A.F. had opened the door for the flowering of my real talent, and, my early brush with the crisis state behind me, it hadn't taken me long to gravitate towards selling. I even spent a couple of early years as a door-to-door salesman, flourishing in the face of the challenges and uncertainties that many people would regard as a daunting way of life.

Later in life I trained other sales people and I can remember trying to instil in them my own feeling for the job. The sales person is akin to the pioneer, to the evangelist, I told them. He is a hero, I maintained, continually breaking new ground, risking rejection and persisting in the face of setbacks, so that everybody else can be secure in their nine to five comfort zones!

It should also be a very honourable calling: although I always worked very hard, for example, I also surrendered the outcome of each day to God, never pushing too hard for business, but confident that my efforts would always meet with a sufficient reward. I felt that every day was a venture into uncharted territory, a journey of trust.

I remember one puzzled housewife trying to express her feeling that I was not really a salesman: "You are just too human," she said. I was in partnership with a friend at the time, selling little hand-made pictures door-to-door, and for the business to work I maintained a discipline that kept me knocking on doors until ten o'clock at night. On one occasion, after a late evening conversation with a couple I had called on, they actually insisted on putting me up for the night rather than allow me to drive the half hour or so back to my lodgings.

On another I was invited to join a Jewish mother and her two young children as they partook of their Friday evening meal for Shabbat. It is, it seems, incumbent upon a Jewish family to welcome in this way anyone who calls at such a time. You can imagine how special that felt. That was more than forty years ago, but I can still see those candle-lit faces in my mind's eye today. This was in Salisbury, and imagine my surprise when the following year I called at the S.P.C.K.[1] bookshop there to offer them a new range of framed pictures of the famous cathedral and found myself face to face with my Jewish friend, who just happened to be the manageress of the store!

I discovered that if I followed Bapak's advice and channelled my heart and mind towards the things of this world, instead of towards spiritual matters, then my latihan became lighter and stronger, clearly benefiting from the non-interference of the thinking. At around the age of thirty I began to take Bapak's guidance about the importance of standing on one's own feet very much to heart. From then on I was always self-employed in one enterprise or another. I invariably chose tough start-up situations calling for a high degree of commitment. I seemed to need a very challenging lifestyle that made enormous demands upon my time and resources, leaving little left over for anything else.

---

[1] Society for Promoting Christian Knowledge.

Typical of these undertakings was a venture into the wine business, challenge enough for a teetotaller who knew absolutely nothing about wine. This opportunity presented itself during a rare period when I was out of work, at a time when we were really up against things financially. It had taken Suzanna and me just ten years to produce six marvellous children, and at this point we were all living in the Subud House in Cheltenham, Gloucestershire. We had no home of our own, no car, very little money, and a flourishing brood of young children to provide for. Things looked so tough that I felt driven to apply for welfare assistance. Yet when the cheque arrived I sent it back. In spite of the apparent hopelessness of our situation, I was reluctant to risk succumbing to dependence on anything other than myself and God. I recognised that a time of seemingly greatest difficulty could also be a time of greatest blessing and opportunity, demanding, as it did, a deeper and truer faith and trust than usual.

When the wine business offer first came my way I turned it down. Klaus had heard about my sales background from a mutual friend and 'phoned from London to ask if I would be interested in setting up an extension of his new wine import business. I explained that, as a non-drinker, I did not really see how I could possibly fit into such a project, thanked him and said goodbye. Three weeks later, and down to our last £20, I felt that I could no longer afford such scruples. I called Klaus and became a wine merchant.

We handled a range of fine French and German wines, and I found it to be a fascinating field of study. I was a comparative newcomer to Cheltenham and knew no-one outside the small Subud community, but, using a friend's telephone, I set up wine tastings at homes and businesses all over town. Within a few months I had created a lucrative network of private customers to whom I would sell large consignments of quality wine by the case. The hardest part in the early days was to project a credible image when I didn't even know what the wines tasted like. I overcame this by listening attentively to the informed comments of my early customers as they sampled the wines, and then advancing these observations as my own when introducing them to others. In this way I soon acquired a totally unfounded reputation for being a wine expert, which was reinforced by a local newspaper article about my activities.

Before long I was able to buy a shop with ample living accommodation, from which Suzanna ran a retail sales department. Our next move was to lease a warehouse and begin to service the local restaurant trade. By this time I was also travelling the country, training others in our modus operandi and helping to set up similar operations. Other areas were not as successful as ours, however, and the company was so overstretched that it could not survive a massive increase in the excise duty levied on wines and spirits in the late 70s.

We moved back to the London area where again, by the grace of God, I enjoyed great success in sales, this time in the field of specialist, high quality cookware.

My motto had become, 'Work as if it all depends on you; pray as if it all depends on God,' and observing the Ramadan fast had also become an increasingly valuable and meaningful way of seeking to maintain that balance.[1]

The Ramadan of 1982 was of particular importance for me, developing into something of a personal retreat after a gruelling eleven years in the direct sales business. Although usually I continued to work during the fast, this time I resolved to let go completely, somehow confident that a new direction would open up for me.

---

[1] Please see Appendix B for clarification as to why so many non-Muslim Subud members adopted the practice of fasting for Ramadan.

'When one door closes another opens' was one of my mother's favourite maxims, one that certainly held true for me at the end of that Ramadan, when Subud brother Andrew Bromley offered me a partnership in a printing company he had started a few years earlier. The business was doing fine but was still quite small and needed a sales boost. The offer was right up my street.

We prospered and within a year we had launched another enterprise, an advertising and marketing agency in partnership with designer Marcus Bolt, another old friend. Before long we had set up a third venture, a typesetting company, joined by yet another old friend, Leonard Hurd, who now runs Subud Publications International. To house our growing group of companies we bought a medium sized commercial building, which, thanks to skyrocketing property prices over the next few years, proved to be an excellent investment.

My own role still encompassed the generation of new business, but a flair for copywriting and the more creative aspects of marketing had emerged and these aspects began to make more and more demands on my time. We were all working long hours, and even Sunday mornings were usually given over to brainstorming our clients' advertising campaigns.

Although Bapak often remarked that we wouldn't begin to realise the true significance and enormity of the blessing we had received with the latihan until after our death, he also said that it would permeate and inform all aspects of *this* life, both inner and outer, that it would be a source of guidance in our work as well as in our spiritual life. I believe that I have been blessed in this way over and over again with the business opportunities and success that came my way. Now, this guidance began to manifest in the creation of advertising concepts. To begin with, I had to cudgel my brain to contribute worthwhile ideas to submit to our clients, but as time went by these would often float effortlessly into my head, sometimes while I was actually sitting across the desk from a client being briefed on the product or service.

I still remember the first time this faculty manifested itself. It gained us one of our biggest clients ever and in so doing served as something of a launch pad for our fledgling agency. The company concerned was the UK branch of a leading American corporation in the field of eye care, and we were given the opportunity of coming up with an ad campaign promoting a new contact lens cleaner. If contact lenses aren't cleaned properly they will acquire a filmy coating that will obscure vision, and we were determined to come up with a striking concept that would make our client stand out from its competitors in the U.K's leading magazine for opticians. By the time I was scheduled to present our ideas to the client, Marcus and I had come up with a dozen or so promising strategies, and I was keyed up to make what would be the first such presentation since my venture into advertising.

That morning I awoke early, way before six, to find myself looking at a screen. Scrolling across the screen were the words, ISN'T IT TIME YOUR PATIENTS STOPPED SEEING DIRTY FILMS? I couldn't believe my eyes! I just knew that this was the perfect solution: an innovative, irreverent approach that would be guaranteed to attract attention in the rather staid professional journal in which the campaign would run.

I immediately called Marcus and by the time we met up that morning he had drawn his usual brilliant visual of the new idea to add to the ones we had already prepared. At the meeting with the company's managing director, I began, one by one, to place the A4 layouts on the desk in front of her, each one offering a different promotional message. She was clearly quite impressed with what she saw, but when I laid down the Dirty Films offering she immediately grabbed it, her eyes sparkling, a big smile on her face. We had a winner, and in due course campaigns like this won an advertising award for our client from the journal concerned, and I was invited to join the M.D. at the presentation ceremony.

By the mid-80s we were making a good living from our Subud enterprises and were able to contribute financially both to Subud and to a few charities. Moreover, the experience of working closely with other Subud members, all of us long-standing friends and all of us subject to our respective purification processes, added a valuable dimension that, although sometimes difficult, was always enriching.

But although things were going well with all three of our business enterprises, as time passed I became aware of an increasing sense of losing my way, if not my very identity. I buried myself even more deeply in my work, but I sensed that an inner confrontation with the negative aspects of my character was again looming large. I felt that I was heading for a momentous personal showdown that nothing would avert. It seemed as though my very selfhood was disintegrating. My life became a desperate struggle to conceal the chaos within and to present a credible front to the world, to family, colleagues and clients alike.

It was around this time, again during the fast of Ramadan, that I had an experience of great significance. The inner self of Marianne, a dear Subud friend of many years, who at that moment lay stricken with cancer and within a week of her death just ten miles away, suddenly appeared in front of me and said, "You will stay at the top till the very end." It was an unmistakable reference to the mountain-climbing dream of so many years before, clearly intended to give me courage and faith in facing what lay ahead.

> **Once you are able to receive clearly in your latihan, your life will be constantly guided by the Power of Almighty God.**
>
> *Bapak*
> *(Talk origin pending)*

5

An Affair of the Heart

Against this backdrop of personal conflict, my weakening marriage suffered a body blow in the early 1980s. Notwithstanding Suzanna's fine character and outstanding qualities as loyal wife and devoted mother, my growing inner turmoil also began to manifest as an emotional vulnerability towards other women. Today, I wonder to what extent this pattern, this desire to please women, might have been due to the fact that as a small boy I lived in a household with no less than four adult women – my mother, grandmother and two aunts. Whatever the driving force behind it, in my early forties I rationalized this tendency with a belief that I needed the 'perfect woman,' a profoundly spiritual lady who would also be capable of satisfying my strongly passionate and sensual nature. Later, I was to receive, "She must first arise within you," but at the time, beset by this deep need and longing, my heart and mind – those potential playgrounds of the low forces – were easily persuaded that my marriage was not 'ideal.' With the benefit of hindsight, I would say that in fact it was exactly that, and that Suzanna was and is among the noblest of women.

Our relationship deteriorated markedly in the late seventies when I began to take a serious interest in Laura. Laura was in her early twenties, about half my age, and we had become good friends while working closely together in business. She was beautiful and spirited, living a long way from her home overseas, and my initial affectionate concern for her well-being developed into love. Before long we had drifted into a full-blown affair despite inner indications to the contrary, which I allowed my 'strong heart' to distort and overrule.

My involvement with Laura can be said to be representative of a mini-series of what some might call 'romantic adventures,' and, knowing that it will alienate some readers, I have debated within myself the need and desirability of touching upon this aspect of my life in this book. On balance, however, I feel that it is right to do so: partly because it is an undeniable aspect of my truth and partly because it may be meaningful to others that despite this weakness of character I was never deserted by the mercy and love of God. I should perhaps add that one of these liaisons resulted in my being rejected by a much younger woman who I loved very much. As a result, I went through a period of heartbreak every bit as devastating as the one I had inflicted upon Suzanna. With hindsight, I am glad this happened: on the one hand, it laid bare a great neediness within me, fertile ground for yet more purification, while, even more importantly perhaps, providing me with an opportunity to discharge a massive karmic debt.

Soon I was in effect leading a double life, leaving home around 9 a.m., seeing as much as possible of Laura during the day and rarely getting home again before 11 p.m. This deceitful regime was facilitated by the fact that my business at that time required me to work most evenings.

Although I wanted to be with Laura, my youngest children were still only in their mid-teens and I could not contemplate leaving the family at that stage. Matters remained unresolved, therefore, while Laura went abroad for a couple of years. We remained in contact, however, and early in 1985 I broached the subject of separation with Suzanna. She was devastated, and

torn between the longing of my heart and my horror at inflict-
ing so much pain upon her, I dropped the subject and did my
best to comfort her.

Six months later, Laura returned to England and we made plans
to move in together. This time, unable to bear witnessing the
suffering I knew it would cause Suzanna, I wrote her a letter of
explanation and left without warning.

I had hoped that this decisive action would help to resolve my
process of inner disintegration. In fact, it only fuelled my dete-
rioration, and I moved through these events as if in a dream. I
bought a small apartment for Laura and myself just west of
London.

Nothing seemed quite real. In the past, I had always been able
to keep the more negative, insecure aspects of my nature under
control through prayer and occasional fasting. Suddenly this was
no longer the case; just the opposite in fact. Now, the slightest
expression on my part of a self-willed prayer or intent to fast, or
indeed to initiate any hitherto ostensibly positive action, would
actually incur the very states they were intended to combat.

It was nearly thirty years since Mary Hyde had received that I
would one day encounter 'a light from far out in space,' and this
is exactly what was now about to happen. It is the first of many
experiences described in these pages that were so extraordinary
as to beggar belief. They were, nevertheless, *real* events, much
more real than our everday reality.

Whatever we receive in the latihan –
because it is all from God
and given by God – cannot be
described or written down on
paper. It is not that it is a secret
or that we are not allowed to
write about it, but someone who
has not experienced or received
what is in the latihan
will not believe it.

Bapak
Vancouver, September 1963
(63 YVR 2)

6

A Light from Space

I awoke in the middle of a night in late October 1986 to find myself instantly wide-awake and standing on a hillside with two unidentified companions.

I looked up and watched with detached interest as a bright light like a shooting star, the most intensely bright light I had ever seen, arched through the sky from deep in space heading towards earth.

The whole episode felt quite natural, and at first I was not at all alarmed. But suddenly I sensed that the light was in some way connected with myself, was in fact heading straight for me. I began to feel afraid.

In my panic I ran behind a nearby wall in the hope of hiding from the fast approaching light. Looking back, I saw that a satellite dish had appeared in the very spot I had just vacated. The dish was so angled that when the light struck it, it ricocheted straight at me, still cowering behind the wall.

The light entered my body and, with one convulsive shudder, expelled the warring forces which, for weeks, had been making my life so miserable.

Immediately afterwards I simply turned over and fell asleep. I awoke in the morning more at peace and at home within myself than I could ever remember feeling.

Surely my ordeal was over?

It had in fact just begun.

7

Crisis

For the next three weeks or so, I was calm and unburdened. My latihan was light and relaxed and the unpleasant inner states did not return.

Yet outwardly I gradually became aware of a mounting sense of lethargy and lack of direction. It was as if I had lost whatever motivating force had driven my life to date. This condition of disorientation came to a climax about a week later.

I was driving on the M1, one of England's busiest motorways, when, without any cause that I could identify, a combination of strange and disconcerting physical symptoms began to manifest themselves. My heart began to pound erratically, my head to swim, and my breathing took on a frenzied rhythm of its own over which I had no control.

Driving became very difficult and, fearing that I might be suffering a heart attack, I pulled over to the slow lane and barely managed to keep going until I reached the family home – only a few miles away – that I had left almost a year earlier. There, my daughters took charge and got me to the local clinic, where my breathing remained wildly irregular and I struggled to remain conscious. Suzanna rushed to join us in time to hear the doctor diagnose my condition as a panic attack. Several injections later and clutching a prescription for tranquilizers, I tottered 'home,' assisted by my anxious family.

Although Suzanna and I had not met for more than a year, she was totally supportive. At the risk of jeopardizing her new-found self-reliance, she agreed that I should stay at the house for a few days while I recovered sufficiently to be able to return to my apartment. The 'children' were now aged between twenty-one and thirty-one, and only the youngest, Ros, was still living at home.

The day after my unscheduled return to my former home, Suzanna drove me into the countryside, where we walked slowly along a riverbank. It was in the stillness of that natural setting that I heard my inner voice say, "Your wife is the one to look after you at this time." In this way, although I had not asked for it, the latihan provided the clearest possible guidance, even in those fraught circumstances. It is a measure of the degree to which my outer life was still dominated by my passions that I chose to ignore it. Once again, my 'strong heart' had the last word, and within a few days I returned to Laura.

The next month or so was a period of limbo, dominated by feelings of weakness at all levels and by a total lack of self-confidence. This condition was probably complicated to some extent by the prescribed drug that I had been given, and I was shown clearly in a dream that the full dose was harmful and should be reduced. I began to cut back on the pills and within a few weeks was able to stop taking them altogether.

At this stage, I was not able to be aware that my breakdown was an integral part of an unfolding spiritual process that would lead to my own inner truth. It was impossible for me to think straight, and I wondered whether the illness might be nothing more than the outcome of years of overwork, coupled with the stress of my unresolved life situation. Needless to say, these were very traumatic weeks for Laura too.

By this time it was becoming clear to both of us that we did not belong together. For my part, I came to see that in following my passions I had been blind to the true interests and will of my inner self. I received that this was why I was now brought so low, and feared that I might have been rejected completely by God as a punishment for my willfulness. This anxiety was at once laid to rest by my inner voice: "There is no question of that, although you must be very careful in the future."

As the process continued to unfold, it became all too evident just how much my own lack of awareness had put me at the mercy of strong animal forces. It was not until years later that I had a very clear dream that was, I felt, an indication that this side of my nature had at last been brought into the right relationship with the inner.

In the dream, I was handling a bull, powerful and dangerous, typical of the bulls I had had to deal with during my time on the dairy farm. But this animal had been dehorned, its massive head completely devoid of those deadly weapons. It came very close to me and lowered its head, and for a moment there was a pulse of anxiety – after all, it could still have beaten me to pulp. All it did, however, was rub its great head gently against me like a cat, its eyes closing in ecstasy as I fondled it. There was a warm loving communion between us.

I felt that this experience dovetailed with Bapak's explanation that in truth the lower forces were intended to be our companions and servants, that it was never God's will for them to dominate our lives.

Meanwhile, Laura and I agreed that a complete break seemed to be the only answer. She moved out, and I remained at the apartment - now, on top of everything else, battling with a great sense of loss at parting from her. We were not to see each other again for two years. We next encountered each other at the 1989 Subud World Congress in Sydney, and it was a great blessing to be presented with this opportunity to heal the wounds and restore a true sister/brother relationship.

Typically, I envisioned recovery as being synonymous with getting back on track in business, and in this vain pursuit I spent a few days at a so-called health farm, a highly prestigious establishment just outside London. There I was allocated a luxury room no doubt previously occupied by a succession of wealthy patrons recuperating from over-exposure to the pressures of business and the excesses of the high life. Whatever the explanation, as soon as I lay down to sleep I was amazed to see droves of hideous, batlike creatures rise out of the bed, expelled by cleansing sheets of beautiful silver rain which fell around me. Strangely, I did not feel disturbed or frightened by the bats; I could only marvel at the grace and beauty of the rain from heaven.

I was grateful that my business partners, Marcus and Andrew, were also in Subud. They stood by me magnificently at a time when I felt as if I were hanging on to my sanity by a hairsbreadth. They insisted that I should feel no pressure about returning to the office. Their patience and forbearance were a lifeline, and they shared much of the emotional distress of those early weeks, as well as many of the powerful latihans I was beginning to experience.

By now it was obvious that I was running around in circles looking for a way out, that I was actually hampering and delaying the smooth progress of whatever God willed for me. I saw, in short, that it was time to surrender. This insight brought with it a glimmering of peace, together with the certainty that I could now begin to leave the outcome completely in God's hands.

A few days later, alone in my apartment, I was suddenly possessed by a condition of personal annihilation, a state of total terror. It was so overwhelming, I felt I would not be able to prevent myself from rushing blindly into the street. But I knew there was nowhere to run. Perhaps I should telephone someone – anyone! But I also knew I would not be able to remember anyone's phone number, let alone dial it.

Then: *No! This time, let me not run; let me experience all that this state has to offer, and let me not be afraid of the fear.* For the first time in weeks, joy and hope began to whisper within me. From deep inside the voice said, "Now you can begin to grow."

Facing my fear was a turning point in my journey to the light.

Changing your soul to one that is
high and noble is not something
you can do yourself, without God's
help. So what you need to do is
simply follow the latihan with
patience, acceptance and
a willingness to let go.

Bapak
Malang, October 1966
(66 MLG 1)

8

Complete Trust and Confidence

It was as if my crisis could now proceed, and somehow it had to be a solitary affair. I still did not know who 'I' was, and relating to others was impossible. I felt transparent, defenceless, and acutely sensitive to what was going on in those around me. For weeks I isolated myself from virtually all contact with others, venturing out only on essential visits to the local shop and to attend group latihan.

I seemed to pass through a period of de-parenting. I had been an only child, sensitive and 'highly strung,' mirroring many of my parents' own characteristics. Also, some of my earliest and most formative years had been spent away from the extreme poverty of my parents' working class environment as the protégé of a group of wealthy benefactors. These good people had committed themselves to giving me a better chance in life than seemed to be possible with parents whose poor financial circumstances were matched only by their poor health.

◆ ◆ ◆

There were three such 'interventions,' and for the life of me I can't recall how my parents would have come to know the three wealthy families involved. That said, all three of them had strong links to the Church of England, so this must have been the common ground that somehow brought them into contact with Mum and Dad.

The first such 'patron' was a kindly and pious clergyman, a Doctor of Divinity connected with Exeter University. Dr. Jalland and his wife lived in a large house in a very well-to-do part of the city. It had its own private chapel, and from time to time I would serve as altar boy while Dr. Jalland said Mass just for the two of us. My most abiding memory of being 'adopted' by the Jallands was my very first full meal with them. I was starving, but when I took my place at the dining table I was so intimidated by the seemingly endless array of silverware in front of me that I told them I wasn't hungry. I just sat there, mouth watering, while they consumed course after course of the most delicious looking food.

Another wealthy lady who took a great interest in me was the equally kindly Mrs. Pennell. She went so far as to offer to pay for me to become a boarder at Exeter Cathedral Choristers School. All I had to do to take advantage of this unbelievably generous offer was to pass a simple singing test conducted by the choir master. As it happens, I do have quite a pleasant singing voice, but when the day came I was so nervous that my vocal chords failed to produce a single sound that could be remotely interpreted as musical.

It seemed that I was destined to continue life as just one of the many disadvantaged kids living on one of the roughest council estates in Exeter.

Then came a third lifeline, this time thrown to me by a lovely lady living alone in a beautiful country retreat on the edge of the picturesque Dartmoor village of Lustleigh. Mrs. Scott was also the local Girl Guide Commissioner, and since there wasn't a Boy Scout pack in the vicinity I became the only male member of her Guide troop, to whose meetings I would wear my

Cub Scout uniform. Needless to say, this involvement would have done nothing to retard the early burgeoning of my interest in the opposite sex, and I recall my especially close friendship with Mavis, one of the village girls.

I can't remember exactly how long I lived with Mrs. Scott – certainly for a year or two – but the idyll ended rather abruptly after my mother was at last able to come and see me. Her visit unsettled me to the point that I became so homesick that Mrs. Scott had no option but to arrange for me to return home. My mother later told me that when I rejoined the family I spoke with such an upper class accent that for a while she and Dad were afraid to open their mouths in front of me!

Looking back through the mists of more than six decades, I am genuinely perplexed as to why this succession of wonderful people should have taken such a positive interest in my welfare. Yes, I was a precocious child – in truth, something of a handful; the sort of youngster who nowadays might even be classified as suffering from ADHD[1] - and perhaps they felt that my undoubted early promise of intelligence merited fostering. A couple of years later, as it happens, I did pass the eleven-plus examination with flying colours and was placed in the top grouping of that year's grammar school three stream intake. Furthermore, in my first term I was actually top of the class, so I must have been pretty bright. It was a very promising start, but before long a penchant for practical jokes and a gift for articulate disrespect towards prefects – sometimes delivered in Latin! - set me on a downward spiral that I just couldn't halt. Once again, I failed to capitalize on a first class opportunity. Instead, I left Hele's School under something of a cloud without having taken any of the usual final exams. In what I came to refer to as my French Foreign Legion act, I joined the Royal Air Force as an administrative apprentice.

---

[1] Attention deficit hyperactivity disorder

◆ ◆ ◆

It was only now, in my early fifties, that I came to see that I had long blamed Mum and Dad for the identity crisis and feelings of inadequacy that had dogged my entire life as a result of those early mixed influences. I had forgotten Bapak's advice that such an attitude was both inappropriate and unnecessary. It was only necessary, he once wrote to me, to have faith in God and a feeling of trust in oneself, the true self that is already a living identity in the womb before falling under the parental and other influences that inevitably beset the growing child. As he put it during a talk in 1967, "This latihan is not new. You already experienced it when you were a baby, when you were in your mother's womb."

Awareness and surrender became my watchwords as experience succeeded experience in what amounted to a virtual re-parenting by the Power of God. It was necessary for me to know and feel that I was truly a child of God, independent of all others. Looking back, I can see that what I am trying to communicate here was perfectly expressed by Bapak during a talk in New York in May 1967: "Thus it could be said that when you follow the latihan you are not the child of a human being any more – you are a child of God. What you got from other people has been removed from you, because what you need comes from God, from your soul."

From this point on, life and latihan began to merge into one continuous flow. The latihan, I became increasingly aware, *is* life. At the end of this phase, I received, "You have already come a long way."

My experiences at this time were symbolized by a graphic dream in which I was brought before a court and accused of many offences. Not only was I found not guilty of all charges, but the judge actually commended me on the *extent* of my innocence. Outside the court I was surrounded by journalists eager to report my story. I eluded them and lowered myself into an underground tunnel that led to an enormous skyscraper just a couple of blocks away. It was a post office depository, crammed with unclaimed letters and parcels. Turning to the reporters, I said, "Do you think I can let matters rest here when I've got *that* to go for?"

I felt sure that the 'unclaimed mail' in the dream must represent unrealized spiritual benefits of some kind: blessings, perhaps, that I had missed out on through reacting against the process and, therefore, blocking my progress in the early sixties. The same Sudarto who had written to me years before when I had just been opened was later to elaborate on this interpretation during conversations in Jakarta, Indonesia, in 1989.

"You yourself are good," he said, "represented by being found innocent by the judge. The undelivered parcels symbolise the inherited impurities of your ancestors, which must also be purified." He pointed out that this new possibility, symbolised by my entry into the underground tunnel, was in itself a highly significant aspect of the experience. Clearly, I had a long way to go!

◆ ◆ ◆

Once my initial panic reaction subsided, the intensive receiving continued for months on end. Now that I was able to go with the process rather than resist it, not a night would go by without the occurrence of one or more inner experiences of one kind or another, often quite startling. In one I received that I was undergoing a 'crucifixion,' and in truth I often felt as if I had to face and accept death within myself in surrendering to whatever the night would bring. This necessity helped to reinforce an attitude of total reliance upon God.

The 'clear dreams' became ever more commonplace. In addition to the more significant messages, most nights I would be shown edited highlights of the events of the next day, which always proved to be accurate down to the smallest detail.

My solitary suffering also continued, as I was led to let go of all previous interests, habits and ways of being. For months, this advertising copywriter, this man whose only spare time interests had been reading complex espionage thrillers and watching comedy and drama on television, was quite unable to write even a postcard, to read as many as two words strung together or to watch anything on TV!

I received that, for me, work had in fact been 'a substitute for *being.*' Now I had no choice but to endure and to *be*, without a moment's escape into fantasy or relaxation.

I felt very much like a newborn child, vulnerable and unfamiliar with the world around me. In fact, I awoke from a doze one afternoon feeling exactly as if I had just been born, as if I had no past. Everything around me seemed so strange and new that I actually went from room to room as if looking at everything for the first time. I even went out in the car to see how the outside world looked. I was surprised that I still knew how to drive!

For a long time, I continued to feel that I no longer had any basis for relating to anyone else on earth. I felt like an alien on this planet, a stranger among its inhabitants, incapable of relationship with anyone other than God. I felt I began to understand what Jesus must have meant when He said, "The Son of Man hath nowhere to lay his head."

One night in a particularly vivid dream, I saw myself being driven slowly to my own funeral. Dressed in a smart business suit, I was sitting calmly upright in the hearse beneath a large banner stretched over my head. It bore the words, 'Complete Trust and Confidence.'

9

Signposts to Renewal

Overall, the period of most intense suffering lasted about two years. During much of this time, fear and despair seemed to reign supreme within me, offering little hope that things would ever be different.

Early on in the process I was shown that my 'learning curve' was necessarily long, gentle and drawn out. I was also shown another's learning curve, and this was steep and comparatively short-lived. The reason for the difference, I was given to understand, was my lack of courage. My recovery was thus a long, slow process of learning to live and be all over again, albeit from an entirely different inner place.

Back in the early sixties, during my first taste of this state, I had had a very clear dream of a 'before and after' nature that had a powerful effect upon me at that early stage in my Subud life. In the first, I was on my knees before Bapak pleading for his help. I was devastated when he totally ignored me as if unable even to acknowledge the existence of a wretch such as me. In the second part, I was clearly much changed and chastened by the passage of time and deliberately remained at the back of a group crowding around Bapak, hoping he would not notice me. This time, however, he singled me out and put his arm around my shoulders. He flashed one of his glorious smiles and said, "Now you are one in heart with Bapak."

Back then, I felt, I had somehow been able to avoid this painful state. Now, some twenty-eight years later, with no choice but to go through it, I experienced a whole series of 'before and after' dreams and visions.

In one, a dream, I had taken my car in for service. It was supposed to be a routine job and at the end of the day I called to pick it up. It wasn't parked with the other vehicles, however, and eventually I found it abandoned on rough ground behind the garage. A mechanic came up to me, shaking his head doubtfully and pointing out all sorts of defects of which I had been unaware.

"You do realize that this car can't last much longer" he said, "No more than a couple of weeks."

"It doesn't matter," I replied lightly. "I'm getting my new one soon."

A week or so later, in latihan, I saw myself out on a hillside with two companions. We looked skyward and saw a brand-new car descending steadily through space. At once my companions began to fit me with a parachute so that I could leap off the earth and glide into the driver's seat as the car floated down.

In another 'before and after' experience, a daytime vision, I saw myself encased in a thick, mummylike outer shell made of lead, a chrysalis-like replica of my whole body. The top had begun to break away, exposing part of my real head. A week or two later, I again saw myself inside an outer skin, also an exact replica, but now it was made of fine porcelain. It was broken away to below my knees, and it would have been a simple matter to step out of it altogether.

I felt that experiences like this were symbolic of the weakening and falling away of the negative aspects of my former self. I remembered one of Bapak's early remarks: "Sometimes when the plant grows the pot breaks."

◆ ◆ ◆

Towards the end of January 1987, a couple of months after my collapse and well before the discernible beginning of a change for the better, I heard a commanding voice in the night say, "He will come on the 16th." Three weeks later, at exactly 8 pm on February 16, I was pulled to my feet by a sudden charge of a very powerful vibration in both arms, for all the world as though both hands were plugged into a high-voltage electrical source. I felt quite frightened as for about fifteen minutes my arms and hands remained rigid, shaking in the grip of this power before the experience settled down into a more normal latihan. Afterwards, I received that this happening was a manifestation of a new and more personal relationship with God. This was one of the first indications I had that something was taking place other than a process of breakdown.

Yet another was a vision in which I saw myself joined by a long silver cord to a much larger and brighter version of myself looking down from above. Then I was the bigger me, smiling down encouragingly at my smaller, ordinary self. I alternated between the two for a while, feeling equally at home as either.

Not long afterwards, I was again visited by the powerful charge of 'high-voltage electricity,' a much stronger version of the fine vibration sometimes felt during the latihan. I was then aware of all desire being expelled from my being, an experience that left me feeling extremely weak and vulnerable for several hours. Later that day, though, I felt uplifted and cleansed, and in that new clarity felt that the only meaningful future work for me would be somehow connected with the spiritual life.

That night I had a particularly vivid dream, in which I flew to Jakarta and was greeted very warmly and intimately by Bapak. He chatted lightly for a while and thanked me for my help before reaching out to shake my hand in farewell. Still holding my hand and with his feet still on the earth, his body stretched way up into the sky and his head disappeared into space.

Thereafter, it seemed that my experiences increasingly pointed to the likelihood that I would one day be used to serve some higher purpose, none more vividly than the vision that followed a dream in which a radiant and dynamic Bapak came to comfort and advise me. He was wearing a bejeweled cloak and a golden headdress. A week later, sitting alone one Saturday afternoon in a quiet, relaxed state, I was suddenly showered from above with jewels, falling softly into place over my shoulders like multi-coloured flower petals to form a cloak. Upon my head descended an ornate headdress. I immediately recognized the cloak and crown as those worn by Bapak in my dream. I looked up, and above my head I saw a knight in full armour astride a magnificent charger.

Sudarto smiled broadly when I told him about this experience. "This means that you have been given a mission by Bapak," he said. "It reminds me of when Bapak used to go off on his travels around the world and leave me in a position of responsibility here in Jakarta. I would wonder how I could possibly fill such a role in his absence. Then I would see myself dressed in a sort of uniform given to me by Bapak and I would know that everything would be alright." He paused. "Your vision of the knight in armour is telling you the same thing: that you will always be given the power to carry through whatever will be required of you."

◆ ◆ ◆

Although someone of the spiritual stature of Sudarto would have no difficulty relating to such experiences, to what is gen-

erally called the rational mind they may well sound altogether
'over the top,' perhaps delusional – certainly overwhelming and
maybe difficult to take seriously. And I can sympathise with that
point of view. I would suggest, however, that they are glimpses
of a reality which is beyond our usual level of consciousness,
one that is accessible only when the individual concerned is in
an extremely quiet inner state, separated and freed from the re-
morseless tyranny of thinking and emotions. In other words,
one needs to be in a subtly altered state to be able to receive
such indications, albeit one based upon surrender and a willingness to let go.

I recall an experience given to someone in just such a state, a
state of latihan in other words, during the very earliest days of
Subud in the West, while Bapak was staying at Coombe
Springs. One afternoon a newly opened woman was standing
in the hallway at the foot of the stairs in the big house; she
happened to look up and saw a blazing sphere of light descending the staircase towards her. It was only when the light drew
level with her that she saw that it was a man – Bapak.

Which reminds me of another story, told to me by Istimah
Week, whom you will meet later in these pages. A friend of
hers had begun to feel rather envious of some of the more
dramatic spiritual experiences happening to one or two of her
Subud friends. "Why don't these things happen to me?" she
would complain. "It's not fair." One afternoon, she was alone at
home, knitting, when she had occasion to get up and open the
door leading into a long corridor. As she began to move into
the corridor she saw approaching her from the far end the figure of Jesus, ablaze with light. "Go away, go away!" she
screamed, and the figure disappeared.

So, yes, if such experiences come our way when we are not
ready for them, they can indeed be overwhelming.

What is important is to be at home,
to be in your own place, which
really means being in your physical
body. It is essential to be at home,
to be in your own place,
so that God can reach you.

Bapak
Jakarta, June 1986
(86 CDK 9)

10

Sudarto

Mas Sudarto Martohudodjo had received the latihan when he was seventeen and, now seventy-four years old – at the time I met him - was the senior of Bapak's original helpers. Over the years, he had earned the respect and gratitude of countless Subud members for the clarity and insight of his receiving and advice.

In 1989, some two years after the most intense phase of my crisis, I travelled to Jakarta and stayed for six weeks at the Subud compound. While there, I was extremely fortunate to be able to spend time with Sudarto during a series of meetings in which I shared with him much of what I had been through, experienced and received. I was also fortunate, given Mas Darto's poor English, that American Subud brother Razid Black kindly made himself available as interpreter at all our get-togethers.

At our first meeting, I told Sudarto that I was writing a book based in part upon my experiences, a book I hoped would reach and speak to 'the outside world.' He received quietly for a moment and then said, "In an age when technology is advancing and morality is declining, this book will help people to feel open. They will feel, 'Ah, here is a way.'"

To my surprise, he continued, seemingly quite out of context, "In general, the economic condition of Subud members is poor at this time. But God is guiding you so that you can help to arrange and strengthen Subud enterprises." His words reminded me of a Ramadan dream of some ten years before in which Bapak took me into his private garden and showed me a small group of newly planted conifers. There were perhaps a dozen altogether, neatly laid out in a semicircle. Each young tree represented a Subud enterprise. "You should be selling all of these," he said to me.

Despite Sudarto's unexpected confirmation of this indication, it was to be over a year before it began to be reflected in my outer life.

The night before my next meeting with Sudarto, I awoke at around 4 a.m. to feel a beautiful latihan entering through the top of my head. The fine vibration then moved down through my body and manifested in a very pure form of sexual arousal that was quite free of desire or passion, that was in fact very sweet and noble and one hundred per cent spiritual in both origin and direction.

Discussing this with Sudarto the following day, he said, "In most cases, sexual union arises from the passions. But, for you at this time, the best time for union is in the early hours of the morning, around 4 a.m., when the passions are at their quietest, but even then *only as a receiving*". He went on to point out that at such times it is best to stay as close as possible to the sleeping state so that, hopefully, the *nafsu* (passions and desires) will not be able to interfere with following the receiving.

"When the inner self is strong enough you can do it when you like," he laughed, "but if you are in doubt as to the source of the impulse to make love, it is better not to pursue it."

Sudarto continued by explaining how a marriage should develop when seen from the spiritual point of view. Although a marriage begins on a heart-to-heart basis, he said, it should then progress to a feeling-to-feeling basis before deepening to an inner-feeling-to-inner-feeling basis and thence to a soul-to-soul basis. He also spoke of this progression in terms of developing from the material level, through the vegetable and animal levels to the human.

Bapak himself often spoke about the quality of received sexual union between husband and wife as potentially the highest form of worship. He explained that when we are no longer controlled by the lower forces, it is possible for the content of our inner feeling to unite with that of our marriage partner and raise it to the level of a complete human being.

Sudarto reaffirmed how much importance Bapak attached to this aspect of the spiritual life, and to the need for the inner self and the latihan to participate, and indeed predominate, in sexual union. He illustrated this inner reality with a reminiscence of a simple but very meaningful anecdote from his own time with Bapak.

They were sitting quietly together one day, both men in the latihan state, while Bapak was smoking a cigar. After a while Sudarto became aware that he was beginning to savour the smell of the cigar, whereupon Bapak immediately cautioned him that he, Sudarto, was beginning to allow his enjoyment of the cigar smoke to eclipse his awareness of the latihan.

◆ ◆ ◆

After his death, my father appeared to me in latihan and summed up this whole question is just four words. "Marriage is very important," he said to me. At the level at which I am writing these words, it is with the deepest regret that, although I believe it is important to share what Sudarto and Bapak said on the subject, I cannot do so as a worthy exemplar. Although I remain on excellent terms with them both, I am divorced, not only from Suzanna but also from my second wife, Maria.

11

The Heart Transplant

On March 25, 1987, I received the most powerful of all the latihan experiences that punctuated this period. It started as a dream but immediately developed into a waking event.

In the initial dream sequence I found myself in an operating room used for heart transplant operations. Two surgeons entered, and to my horror I realized that I had been cast in the role of patient. I protested vigorously that it must be a mistake, but the surgeons ignored my pleas and prepared to operate. One had a very long strip of adhesive tape across his own chest on the outside of his rubber gown, and I knew this signified that he himself had once been the subject of just such an operation. Both took great interest in inspecting the surgical instruments, and one said to the other, "I wonder whether they still do things the way we used to in our day."

At this point I awoke and was able to see right up into the night sky, the walls and roof of my bedroom having completely disappeared. I saw two angels descending to earth carrying between them an enormous heart, complete with trailing arteries. The organ itself was about two-thirds as big as the angels. And it was transparent; I could see right through it to the stars beyond. I wondered what it could be made of, and a voice answered, "Diamond."

I closed my eyes and soon felt the onset of a very powerful vibration in my chest, yet another charge of 'high voltage electricity.' I felt afraid and was sure I must be dying from a heart attack. But, because I was quite alone and knew there was absolutely nothing I could do about the situation, I was able to relax my body and surrender everything to God.

For some time in latihan I had been receiving a progressive state of surrender to what I can only call the attributes of God. 'I surrender to the grace, majesty, wisdom and perfection of the One Almighty God; I surrender to the will, purpose and magnificence of the One Almighty God; I surrender to the joy, happiness and beauty of the One Almighty God,' and so on, demonstrating, I felt, that all things truly good and noble can come only from Him. I was now aware of these attributes flowing into my chest.

After a while the vibration stopped and I lay still, feeling as weak as I could imagine anyone feeling while still alive. Then I found myself looking down on my body lying on the bed, clothed like a knight crusader in a white tunic bearing the red cross of St. George.

Next, despite my weakness, I was compelled to get out of bed and was somehow 'walked' into the next room. There I was made to kneel and prostrate myself in prayer before being returned to bed. Before falling asleep, I saw in the darkness above me a knight in armour astride a magnificent horse.

◆ ◆ ◆

"Did things begin to improve for you after this experience?" asked Sudarto during our talks in Jakarta two years later. "Yes," I replied, "That's exactly what happened."

12

Ave Maria

A few days after the 'heart transplant,' I received, "It is now God's will that you become well and strong by being peaceful and quiet."

Later that same day, quite unexpectedly, I received, "Maria will lead you on. She will guide and strengthen you." From that time on the feeling of a growing relationship with Our Lady, the mother of Christ, became an increasingly significant aspect of my latihan. At other times too I was aware of her nearness and guidance. Her name would constantly arise within me.

Bapak always attached great importance to a person's name, maintaining that it should reflect inner reality. During his lifetime, therefore, it had long been the practice for Subud members to ask him for their 'right' name, a responsibility and capacity that passed to Ibu Rahayu, Bapak's eldest daughter, in the year before his death.

Around this time, aware that I was undergoing a process of great change, I wrote to Bapak and asked for a new name.[1] The

---

[1] See Appendix B for an explanation as to why some Subud members choose to change their name.

reply, which came from Ibu Rahayu, was 'Marius,' the masculine form of 'Maria.' It was wonderful to have this precious link reinforced in this way. Much later, I visited the scenes of Our Lady's apparitions at Fatima, Portugal, Guadaloupe, Mexico, and Garabandal, Spain, and in all three places this inner connection was reaffirmed in strong and beautiful latihans.

Nevertheless, not long after receiving my new name, while going about my everyday life, I suddenly heard Bapak's voice loud and clear in my ear saying, "Then, I will tell you your *real* name." From that moment on, although I loved the name Marius and would have been happy to bear it for ever, I knew that one day it would change. I began to feel that somehow it was a temporary support, an outward expression of Our Lady's inner help during the time of my extreme weakness.

◆ ◆ ◆

My own family had long had good reason to revere the person of the Virgin Mary.

Some seventy years ago my father had been seriously ill with tuberculosis, a killer disease in those days. Major surgery seemed inevitable, and a successful outcome was by no means certain. My mother, a devout Anglican Christian, had heard of the Shrine of Our Lady at Walsingham, Norfolk, widely known as a place of pilgrimage and healing.

It is recorded that in the year 1061 Mary appeared to Richeldis, the lady of the manor, and asked that a church be built in her name at Walsingham, close to a stream of pure water. It was Mary's wish that the church should be a re-creation of the 'Holy House' where she received the news from the angel Gabriel that she was to be the mother of Jesus. This was duly accomplished, and Walsingham, often referred to as 'England's Nazareth' became the focus of centuries of worship and intercession.

To make the journey from our home in Devon in South West England to Norfolk was no small matter for my parents. Dad was weak from his long illness, and the family was very poor. We could afford to have chicken just once a year as a real treat, for example, which, needless to say, was on Christmas Day. Mum was determined, however, and after weeks of prayer and preparation they somehow managed to scrape together the money to pay for the trip.

When they finally reached the tiny Norfolk village, they were both immediately absorbed into the serenity that pervades the area, which for most visitors is a significant blessing in itself. Nowhere is this concentration of peace and spirituality more palpable than in the Holy House, the inner sanctum of the Shrine. There, after drinking from the ancient well, my parents knelt together in prayer. Neither could speak at this time. It was only later, sitting together in the tranquility of the adjacent garden, that they realised they had both undergone an identical experience at the altar. Both had been aware of a sensation of dizziness, accompanied by what they both described as 'a sort of shivery feeling,' an expression I was occasionally to hear used in later years to describe the vibration of the latihan.

After a week's stay in Walsingham they returned home, and Dad kept an appointment for more X-rays and other tests prior to the planned readmission to hospital. To the amazement of the doctors, his lungs were now clear and it was quite unnecessary for him to have surgery.

Furthermore, although my mother had had only my father's healing at heart in planning the pilgrimage, she herself had been a long-time victim of diabetes. Her doctor was also in for a surprise when she too was discovered to be completely free of her illness. She was immediately able to discontinue treatment and remained clear of the disease for the rest of her life.

From that time on, Walsingham occupied a central place in my mother's devotional life, and occasional visits to the village were highlights of the remainder of her days. She often said that, for her, it represented the nearest thing to Heaven on earth.

She died very suddenly in 1987 at age seventy-seven, in peace and contentment, keenly looking forward to yet another visit to Walsingham which we had been planning as a special treat for her just a few days later.

Without knowing it, I had been prepared for her death in a dream about two months earlier. In the dream, I was walking beside a high wall along a tree-lined road with someone whose face I couldn't quite see. Suddenly, this unidentified person turned to me and said, "There's nothing to it. By the time I hit the ground it will be over." In the event, the road on which Mum was to collapse and die so suddenly a few weeks later proved to be the one I had seen in my dream. And when I spoke to the hospital nurse, she said, "It might be of some comfort for you to know that your mother would not have suffered at all."

By an extraordinary 'coincidence' a feeling of deep inner connection was re-established between Mum and me in the few days before her death. Whereas our contact up until that point had for some time been limited to one dutiful weekly phone call, for some reason I was moved to phone her on each of the four days immediately prior to her passing. Our conversations became progressively lighter, and during one of these calls I played her a short extract from a CD I had bought especially for her to listen to while staying with us after the projected trip to Walsingham. It was Handel's Messiah, her all-time favourite, which I had also come to love as a child.

I turned up the volume and held the phone away from me so that she could hear the music. When I held the receiver to my ear again, it was to hear her voice soaring with the glorious strains of the Hallelujah Chorus. In that same instant I felt joined to her in a deep thrill of joy and reconciliation.

That night I experienced a very strong dream latihan in which, imbued with great spiritual power and wielding a mighty sword, I was cleansing the Shrine at Walsingham as if in preparation for an event of significance. This is the only dream that I have had relating to Walsingham, and I did not receive any indication as to its meaning. But forty-eight hours later my mother was dead, and a week later I had a vision of her walking in the gardens of the Shrine of her beloved Lady.

◆ ◆ ◆

My own feeling of the nearness of Mary continued to deepen. I re-visited Walsingham, and walked alone through the village my parents had loved so much. In the Shrine I experienced the oneness between my latihan and the spirituality of Mary, and I received that she is 'the Queen of all nations.' I also received, "He has built within you a cradle for His love," beautiful words I was to have good cause to remember in October 1989 when I visited Medjugorje in the former Yugoslavia, scene of Our Lady's most recent and frequent apparitions. While there I experienced a Love beyond description.

> **The true situation of man in his worship of God is not that he should create, direct or concentrate on anything, but only receive whatever may be bestowed upon him.**
>
> *Bapak*
> *London, August 1959*
> *(59 LON 5)*

Bapak

Photo courtesy of Simón Cherpitel

Mark Week

Istimah Week

Photos courtesy of Sandra Week

My father, Stanley, pictured in the garden of the Anglican Shrine of Our Lady of Walsingham, Norfolk, England

My mother, Evelyn, at the head of a procession inside the Shrine at Walsingham. Dad died in 1976, and on the back of this photograph Mum wrote: 'May 1977. My first Pilgrimage without Stan.'

The author at age 16.

The author in 2009, aged 72.

13

A New Brain

By now, many of my inner experiences began to take me into space. The first of these happened one Sunday morning when, feeling a little weak and disoriented, I had gone to lie down. Suddenly, I found myself high above the earth, looking down on the hazy beauty of the curve of its horizon far below. I looked up and a slit appeared in what I knew was the outer perimeter of this material world. I might have expected such an astounding, wide-awake experience to be disturbing and frightening, but it was its natural quality that was so significant. I felt so free, light and at home up there. It was returning to the body afterwards that felt awkward and alien.

I came to welcome the feeling of effortless travel beyond the confines of this world, a state in which I began to feel increasingly secure and at home. Once I saw myself in orbit around the earth, exactly like a satellite. The satellite was not yet operational, however, as if waiting for mission control to throw a switch. At other times during this phase I could be blissfully cruising through space in this condition in my inner being while, at the same time, on the ordinary level, driving the car on auto pilot. Would this qualify as multi-tasking, I wonder!

In the middle of the night of April 2, 1987, I found myself instantly wide awake and aware that something important was about to happen. A commanding voice announced, "Prophet Muhammad," and although I couldn't see anyone I was at once aware of his presence in the room.

Without any preliminaries we left this world and travelled deep into space, on and on. On all sides, and for as far as the eye could see, we were surrounded by a myriad stars of varying size and intensity, just like the cover of this book. Although the distance involved was vast by earthly standards, the journey did not take long. I was fully conscious and aware of a faint whooshing sound. Eventually we came to a halt and stood together gazing at an enormous edifice, majestic and impenetrable, still farther out in space. I was not told what it was. After a while I said in awe, "No-one can look at this for too long," and we turned back.

During the return journey, the Prophet Muhammad (upon whom be peace) confirmed that my relationship with Laura had indeed been an error and that this must stand corrected. I felt quite calm and normal throughout this entire experience, although it was to be several months before I would be given any clue as to the nature of the structure I had been taken so far to see.

I continued to be very weak. It was as if I was undergoing a protracted period of convalescence, one that amounted to a training course in complete surrender. I had to have immense patience during this phase. I still could not read or watch television, and listening to music became all-important to me. The slightest exertion would shatter my tenuous hold on physical health. I would often overreach my limited strength and feel lost in a kind of no-man's-land of weakness.

Then, one night, I was visited by two unidentified figures. They bent over me, and one of them held a mirror to my lips to see if I was still breathing. In the morning, I awoke to hear a voice saying, "It has come to our attention that you are very weak right now. But we are here to tell you that you will become very, very strong in the future."

Discussing all this with Sudarto later, his comment may well seem strange to our Western minds. "It is quite usual," he said, "for angels to work in pairs."

A few weeks further into my convalescence, in an early morning latihan, I was taken by the same two companions to choose a new computer. "How nice it would be to have a modern one," I said. "Don't worry," they replied, "It will be the most up-to-date model available – all in one piece."

That night I awoke to observe my two visitors bolting the new computer into my head. "You'll need a week or so to get used to it," they said, and for the next few days I was aware of an unfamiliar, slightly dizzy sensation in my head.

I recognized my 'new brain' as soon as I saw it. It was an exact replica in miniature of the edifice I had been taken into space to see some two months earlier by the Prophet Muhammad.

> By God's Will, the training of
> the soul is self-acting
> and proceeds spontaneously.
> You do not need to
> think about it.
>
> *Bapak*
> *(Talk origin pending)*

14

Back in Action

My return to work was a slow process, and at first I could only manage a couple of hours a day. Gradually this increased to half days and eventually to a full working week.

Not that I ever returned to anything like my former total involvement with business. Now I was content to work shorter hours, and I also worked differently. I was no longer *identified* with work. Instead, I remained tuned to what I came to regard as a spiritual pacemaker, an inner regulator that kept everything in its right place and in perspective.

With my new 'brain' had come a file drawer crammed full of computer programs. The first two related to an important meeting scheduled for a week later. Our most important client at that time had been taken over by a larger group, so that a sizeable percentage of our turnover was at risk. The new owners would, after all, have their own agency, and it would be my job to persuade the new management to retain our services.

In terms of dealing with the outside world, this would be my first really tough challenge since my collapse, and I was by no means confident that I was ready for such a confrontation. On entering the boardroom it became at once apparent that the situation was even more daunting than I had anticipated. I could see that I was in real danger of being caught in the cross-fire between rival management cliques, each fighting for supremacy, if not for their very survival, in the executive shake-up that often accompanies corporate takeovers.

I sat nervously through the preliminaries, feeling vulnerable and unsure of myself after the trauma of the past year. I was all too aware of the dark undercurrents of anxiety, conflict and ambition in the room, and of the marked hostility on the part of two men in particular towards the potential threat I represented to their roles and to their established ways of doing things. Then it was my turn to be introduced by the chairman as he casually threw me to the lions.

I looked around the room without a thought in my head and with no notes to work from. Suddenly, it was as if my new brain switched into action. I felt filled with power and clarity. To my amazement and relief, I gave the performance of my life. I observed myself knitting the meeting together, smoothing ruffled feathers along the way, and delivering a brilliant presentation of our company's irreplaceable expertise and experience in what I perceived to be the exact area of their greatest need.

By the time I finished, all present were in agreement that no other agency could possibly handle their immediate requirements. Winding up the meeting, the chairman thanked me for contributing such a refreshing combination of enthusiasm and professionalism.

Phew!

In fact, this proved to be the first of many similar incidents in the year ahead, in which an increasingly relaxed and dispassionate stance based upon the latihan went hand in hand with success and effectiveness in business. Our creative marketing solutions would invariably meet with the instant approval of our clients, and this apparently effortless success called to mind the encouraging advice given by Icksan (one of Bapak's earliest helper-ambassadors to the West) not to be afraid of letting go of existing powers in order to be able to regain them from a higher level.

The year following my return to the office proved to be our most successful ever. Although I had many other commitments, I was able to bring in more new businesses than all our three sales representatives put together. This success came very easily and I did not feel I could take personal credit for it. I knew that it was due entirely to God's blessing and guidance.

Actually we should not say the
spiritual exercise 'of Subud.' It makes
it sound as if it is only in Subud that
you can receive God's grace, the guidance
of God, or the revelation of God.
Which is not the case.
The fact is that anyone who surrenders
to God with patience, acceptance and
sincerity can receive the latihan.
It is not the 'copyright' of Subud.
Nobody can lay claim to God.

Bapak
Jakarta, June 1985
(85 CDK 8)

15

The Punch

"May this 'I' die, and may another live in me greater than I and better for me than I."

– St. Teresa of Avila

It was at this point in the regeneration process that I received that I had experienced the end of a life and death cycle. It was certainly true that I had gone through a death or separation in relation to my former self and ways of being, evidenced by character changes that one of my business partners was later to describe as 'huge.' In addition to the transformation of my attitude towards work, for example, I could no longer swear, touch alcohol – fortunately, I was no longer in the wine business! - tell or listen to tasteless jokes, or look at women in an inappropriate way, all of which had in varying degrees hitherto been habitual to me.

Then, I had a dream that seemed at first entirely without reality, little more than a source of amusement. Eventually, however, I came to recognise the far-reaching significance of its inner meaning. I came to see that it was laying down the ground rules that would govern every second of my existence for the rest of my life. It was a pivotal experience, one that could easily provide the theme for an entire book, a book without an ending since it goes to the very heart of staying close to the spiritual life, our true home, while still in this world, this homeland of the lower forces.

In the dream, I had just finished cleaning out an enormous cowshed, and it looked spotless. My boss came to inspect my work. "So you're satisfied with this, are you?" he asked me.

I looked around again but could see nothing to complain about, unless you counted a single tiny piece of straw lying at my feet. But even that was perfectly clean and shiny. It looked exactly like a small golden capital letter *I*.

"Come and have a cup of tea," said my boss, in a very friendly manner.

Over tea, he said, "From now on, whenever it is appropriate for you to say either 'please' or 'thank you' to me, you must say it *immediately*."

Sounds easy enough, I thought to myself.

A few minutes later such an occasion arose, and I was in the process of formulating the best way to say 'thank you' when, without warning, my boss drew back his fist and punched me in the jaw without warning, knocking me over backwards.

"I said *immediately*," he reminded me.

Before long, the crucial message represented by this dream began to get through to me: that it was vital to stay very close to the fountainhead of an emerging new spiritual identity; that through awareness I must allow this higher level to govern every act and movement, every thought and intention, and every usage of the senses.

I began to experience that only through constant attention from moment to moment would this inner contact and balance be maintained. If my awareness slipped, even for an instant, I would pay a heavy inner price, aptly symbolized by the punch in the dream. The slightest inattention in any part of my being – even, for example, a tiny careless movement of a little finger, a movement in which a personal intent might predominate – would be enough to trigger one of these 'awareness slips,' as I came to call them.

This very difficult period lasted for some years. It was like walking a tightrope or skating on very thin ice during every waking hour. Constant inner attention was called for, a faculty which seems normal now. As Bapak wrote in *Susila Budhi Dharma*:

> ... so if a man is inattentive, even for just a moment, then he will instantly become unable to tell one from another of the forces that impose on his inner feeling at such a time.

The process intensified as the demands of this inner awareness extended to my freedom to speak in the first-person pronoun, which was gradually withdrawn from me altogether. Strange and hard though this seemed, I simply had no choice but to accept and follow what was now clearly more than ever a continually unfolding process.

Bizarrely, during the first phase of this new trial, I found that if I said the word *I* (or any other personal pronoun) before 8.45 a.m. or after 5.45 p.m. (i.e., outside normal business hours) I would at once become heavily oppressed by negative lower forces. Such an utterance, I came to see, equated with an 'awareness slip' and brought with it a highly unpleasant condition that could last for several hours and sometimes for a whole day. After being allowed a few weeks to get used to this, the restriction was extended to include weekends. Once I had adjusted to that, it was further extended so that I was bound to this extraordinary discipline around the clock seven days a week.

Except when it arose of itself in latihan, I was unable to use any personal pronoun whatsoever – *I, me, my* or *mine* – for more than a year, a requirement that called for an unbelievable degree of self-awareness. I became adept at conducting conversations without using personal pronouns, speaking of myself either in the third person or in the first person plural when absolutely necessary. Naturally, I felt very self-conscious about this at times, especially when talking to strangers. Once, when booking a travel reservation, the clerk asked me, "So how many people are actually travelling, sir?" One day I was accosted by a Frenchman in Carmel, California, who asked me the way to the beach. Thinking it would be safe to let my guard down when speaking French, I relaxed and replied at length using *je* and *moi*. Big mistake!

During this time I was somewhat comforted to come across the following remark made by Bapak in Jakarta in August 1973:

> Bapak hopes that you will truly surrender to God Almighty and give up your *I,* so that your *I* can be stripped bare and you can receive what is actually there in your inner self.

And by another he made in Vancouver in July 1981:

> The word *I* is a very important thing to have and use. But if you misunderstand it or misuse it, or if you are not clear about it, then it can also be very dangerous, because we say all the time, "I do this" or "I do that" or "I am able to know this, and say that, and do that."
> But who is 'I'?
> When we say *I,* it is not at all easy; it is very difficult to be clear who is *I* and who is influencing *I* at that moment.

He went on to explain that the purpose of the latihan is to teach us to experience the separation of our real *I* from all the subordinate forces – the material, vegetable, animal and ordinary human levels of being – that vie for ascendancy within us.

Thankfully, the period without the everyday use of the personal pronoun is now long behind me, and it should be said that I do not know of any other Subud member who has been subject to such a curious and exacting constraint. Needless to say, however, this question of the separation of true identity from the array of imposters and poseurs arising from the lower forces is an unending process.

For years now, the word "I" has arisen of itself within my inner being, but possessed of a purity and newness quite unlike one's normal usage of the personal pronoun. As time passed, this simple expression has evolved into "I am," into "I am God," into "I love," or "I am Love," into "I am the one who is coming," etc.

All such variations emanate from the same clear source, a place that is increasingly accessible in any moment of quietness and surrender, and often – more unexpectedly – by way of the reassertion of inner sovereignty in moments of sudden awareness of having fleetingly and unwittingly become identified with a mundane manifestation of thought or feeling.

It would be easy for the ordinary mind to be alarmed or confused at such inner pronouncements, to fear perhaps that one is going crazy. It would even be possible for the ego to take it personally and begin to build up a fantasy world for itself.

I know that I am not alone in experiences of this kind, and perhaps others will find it helpful and reassuring, therefore, - as I did - to read the following extract from a talk given by Bapak in The Hague as far back as 1957:

Knowing the real 'I' means the same as saying 'I know God.' Such a saying, however, is very difficult to analyse. It is very hard to comprehend it without misunderstanding, because it is not yet known, it has not been experienced yet, what the condition within the human spirit is, so that it may be believed and concluded to mean, 'To know me is to know God.'
"It could even give the idea that God may be just like me, or that God may be just like Bapak, for instance. What is really meant is nothing of the sort, but rather, whoever knows 'I,' or when I know 'I,' it means the same as 'I know God.'

This truth was also attested to in 2003 by Dr. David R. Hawkins in his book *I*:

To surrender identification with that which was presumed to be 'me' allows the real Me to shine forth as the immanent quality of Divinity that is the source of the unencumbered reality of 'I.'[1]

---

[1] Page 220, *I: Reality and Subjectivity* by David R. Hawkins, MD, PhD, published 2003 by Veritas Publishing, www.veritaspub.com.

16

Interlude and Asides

In January 1989 I travelled alone to Sydney, Australia, for the Subud World Congress, held every four years. Although I felt inwardly detached and without expectation at the prospect, I also knew that I had to go. In the event, I was agreeably surprised when the trip turned into a magical two weeks of receiving and sharing with 1,500 Subud brothers and sisters from all over the world. For me, the journey culminated in a four-day stopover in Jakarta on the way back home and a visit to Bapak's grave. The concentration of sheer spiritual power pervading the site was in itself worth all the travelling involved. Curiously, I had never visited Indonesia during his lifetime.

While at the Congress, one particular experience served to underline just how sensitive I had become. During my stay I met up with old friend Robert Wilton, a fellow former member of the Loudwater Group who had been living in Australia for a while. We spent a day together during a trip to the Blue Mountains, a great opportunity for catching up on our news. He mentioned in passing that a friend of his had recently committed suicide in a rather bizarre way. It was little more than a passing reference and he didn't elaborate upon the actual method of his friend's death.

Back in my room at the end of the day I stood to do my usual 'rinsing out' latihan before going to dinner. To my astonishment, I immediately found myself engulfed in flames. There was no pain of course and the experience was over in seconds. I had no idea what to make of it. The next day I bumped into Robert again and told him what had happened. "That's extraordinary," he said, "because that's how my friend killed himself. He doused himself with petrol and set fire to himself."

I felt that this little experience was a graphic reminder of how words have the power to convey their actual content to the listener. It's hardly surprising, therefore, that the great religions warn us against indulging in gossip and other forms of verbal negativity. Who knows what toxicity and heaviness we are contributing to what, as far back as 1962, renowned multi-disciplinarian and Pulitzer Prize-winner Ernest Becker called 'the pathology of normalcy' when we do so. Surely, too, we need to be on our guard against over-exposure to the non-stop onslaught of our modern media, with its 24 hours-a-day bad news bulletins and 'reality' shows.

Sadly, I also learned the hard way that much that passes nowadays for 'spirituality' is in fact highly questionable. Laid up with flu one day while living in New Mexico, a friend very kindly loaned me a video containing hours of unedited footage he had shot of a couple who have since become very well known for their channelling of a particular 'entity.' "This'll help to pass the time," he said, and I happily settled down to watch the film. The first few minutes, during which the couple chatted together about how this phenomenon had come to assume such importance in their lives, were fine. Then came the moment when the woman switched from her everyday mode into the trance-like state that would enable her to become a channel. She began to speak in an altered voice, and in that same second I experienced a blinding pain in my head and instinctively threw myself across the room to switch off the video player.

The salutary lesson here is that, although this so-called 'entity,' purportedly a venerable and revered Biblical figure, speaks in words of sweetness and light, I feel I have good reason to believe that it is in fact a manifestation of a very low force.

I would also agree with David Hawkins, a genuine voice of enlightenment in our time and author of *Power vs Force* and a string of other remarkable books, that we need to be very cautious about exposing ourselves to the questionable influences pervading some New Age stores. Again, I speak from experience. For seven years from the year 2000, I lived alone in Budapest, Hungary, where I was in the habit of visiting a particular health food store. One day the business changed hands and when it reopened it was being operated by a society affiliated with a famous modern Indian guru. I went along to the store as usual and as I passed a section given over to this man's books and videos I was at once aware of being assailed by a highly malevolent force. For days thereafter I struggled in latihan with this invader, and it was only when I accepted the situation and sincerely surrendered that it left me. Interestingly, there was no great drama involved with its departure: "Okay, I'm going now," it said to me, and left with a whisper.

◆ ◆ ◆

One incident, something of a minor miracle, served to demonstrate that although there were occasions during my journey when I felt very alone and abandoned, I was in fact always accompanied by the Power of God and that this protecting contact was always just a hairsbreadth away.

At the time, my second wife, Maria, and I were living in Montana, on the shores of the Flathead Lake, the largest lake west of the Mississippi and in the shadow of the majestic Glacier National Park. I had applied for the much coveted Green Card that would authorize my permanent stay in the United States, and we had been summoned for interview in Billings, the State capital. There was only one problem; well, two actually.

For the past three months, unable to speak a word, I had been reduced to communicating with Maria by way of scribbled notes on scraps of paper. When 'talking' with friends on the phone I would tap out a greeting on the handset. Now this was a bizarre enough state of affairs on its own, but it was compounded by the fact that neither could I read a word. A touch typist, I would work on the computer with the screen covered with a cloth and at meal times I would ensure that all sauce bottle labels, for example, were tuned away from my line of vision. When driving, I would have to turn my head away from locking on to advertising hoardings and the like.

How on earth could I attend a searching interview with the Immigration and Naturalization Service while maintaining a stoic silence and declining to read and complete a few forms?! I couldn't see how I could possibly go through with it, but, despite these minor challenges, 'testing' indicated that all would be well.

The interview was scheduled for 10 a.m. and since Billings was about a four hour drive from home, we decided to make the trip the evening before and stay in a motel so as to be fresh for the ordeal. Our motel was just a short drive from the I.N.S. office, and although I felt quite at peace as we got into the car I still couldn't speak. Then, after a few minutes, I found myself beginning to whisper to Maria and then to croak the first words to pass my lips in three months. By the time we reached our destination I was talking normally, and as we walked up the steps of the government building I can still remember laughing and joking as if I hadn't a care in the world. It really did feel like a minor miracle, but it wasn't over yet.

When we were ushered into the presence of the official whose job it was to conduct the interview, we found ourselves face to face with a man in some distress. Holding his head in both hands, he explained that, for the first time in his life, he had a blinding migraine headache and could barely see, let alone think straight. "Just sign here," he said, pushing a complicated form across the table. I didn't have to read a word in what must have been the shortest I.N.S. interview ever!

I share this anecdote because I feel it perfectly epitomises a later receiving to the effect that, "You will always be taken care of in every way," which has certainly continued to be the case right up until this very day. As to the purpose and benefits of my time without a voice . . . well, with the ordinary mind I cannot know these for certain. In my case, the discipline was imposed upon me, although there are of course numerous examples of monastic orders that voluntarily embrace a vow of silence. Certainly, it was a time of deepening inner awareness and focus.

I digress, but having done so I feel it would be remiss of me not to share with you two profound and heart-warming stories connected with the passing of the contact from one person to another, reminiscences that would otherwise go entirely unrecorded. The 'opening' is an entirely unique experience for everyone, and both anecdotes illustrate that, regardless of how little may appear to be happening in the outer world of our senses, inwardly, in the usually unseen spiritual realm, great things are being accomplished.

The first story concerns Frank, Maria's stepfather. During World War II, Frank had been a forward observer for an American artillery unit in the drive north through Italy. His job was to go ahead of the main force, spot enemy concentrations and radio back their position so that the heavy guns could zero in on their targets. Climbing alone through a mountain pass one day, Frank rounded a bend in the path to find himself face to face with a solitary German soldier, probably engaged upon the same sort of mission. It was a case of kill or be killed, and a hand-to-hand fight between the two combatants was unavoidable. Frank triumphed, but at a psychological cost that one can scarcely imagine, and the horrific memory of this fight to the death haunted Frank from that day on.

At his opening in Boston, Massachusetts, decades later, Frank found himself reliving the entire experience, but this time both he and his opponent were bathed in sheets of silver rain that transformed both of them. Thereafter, the traumatic memory of the event was entirely healed within him.

The second incident concerns Walter, whose opening I witnessed in southern New Mexico where Maria and I started several new Subud groups in the early 1990s. Walter's story is a beautiful illustration of the truth of what Bapak said about the latihan also lifting up and benefiting both our forebears and our descendants. At this first latihan, Walter stood stock still throughout the entire half hour, seemingly experiencing nothing. After the latihan, he left immediately, clearly not wishing to talk. A week later, during our next visit just this side of the Mexican border, Walter took me aside and asked, "Would you like to know what happened during my opening?"

"The first thing you have to know is that my dad and I had had a falling-out, so that when he died about a year ago we hadn't spoken for some time. I felt real bad about this.

"Then, six months ago, my son was killed in a road accident and the same thing had happened. We had had a disagreement and hadn't spoken for a long time. You can imagine how I felt about all this.

"During my opening, though, I saw Dad sitting in a chair with my son standing beside him. Both of them were smiling and holding out their arms to me, and I just knew that everything was okay between us."

The latihan is truly a gift beyond price.

◆ ◆ ◆

During the closing weeks of 1988 I had begun to find it increasingly difficult to identify with the interests and aspirations of our advertising clients. It was as if a switch had been turned off inside me. I felt I must be approaching a major change of direction, and several inner 'hints' seemed to suggest that this would be connected with going to America. I had shared this uncertainty with Andrew and Marcus, promising them a firm decision about my future with the company by the time I returned from Congress.

Although I had never been a diarist, before leaving the U.K. I had been moved to pack a large notebook with a view to keeping a journal of my time 'down under.' Instead, within hours of arriving at Congress, and completely out of nowhere, I felt a strong impulse to begin to write about my experiences of the past two years, which I had kept very much to myself. I spent my first five days and nights in Sydney in something of a creative fever, producing the first draft of the manuscript that was eventually to develop into this book.

In a Ramadan dream of some years before, I had stood beside a very animated and enthusiastic Bapak, facing a group comprising what might be termed the 'Subud establishment.' Bapak called me *Parousia,* a name that meant nothing to me at the time and which was to remain a mystery for another decade. Then, pointing at me, Bapak said, "This is the man to tell the world about Subud."

At the time, as an obscure Subud member immersed in business and the hard-working father of six children, I could not begin to see how such an indication could ever become a reality, although I could not doubt the truth of its inner meaning. Now I connected it with my writing, and I knew that I had to be free to follow my inner guidance and focus on this book. As soon as I returned to England, I withdrew from my business partnerships.

17

Forward in the Light

It was impossible at this stage for my thinking mind to under-stand the spiritual reality of what had happened to me during my crisis. The true spiritual realm, after all, is beyond man's or-dinary understanding and can only be experienced and related to when the mind and heart are set aside. But it was impossible *not* to see that the process had brought about a complete change of inner being, or at least a change of the ruling power within.

Yes, it had also been a time of great weakness and incapacita-tion, but at a particularly low point I had received, "You will be restored to *His* strength," reminding me of the lovely aphorism from 2 Corinthians: 'My strength is made perfect in weakness.'

Beginning to emerge from the crisis state, I was fascinated to observe that it was necessary for me to receive from within how to move all over again in latihan, almost as if I were be-ginning my spiritual training from scratch. It took me several weeks, for example, simply to be able to stand upright again and to begin to take short, tentative steps. It was months before I could move really freely again in latihan: to walk, to run, to dance, to laugh, to sing.

With the most severe phase of the crisis behind me and my book taking shape, constant prayer would arise effortlessly of itself within my being – not as the product of my will, heart, mind and intent, but as the natural flowering of the inner self. Just as a star expresses God's grandeur, a flower His delicacy and beauty, a tree His majesty, an animal His very aliveness and spontaneity by just *being* what they are, so a true human being, it seemed to me, should be a *natural* expression of His love and nobility.

Every day my inner self would pray, "I am so happy and joyful in your presence. You are so wise and wonderful. Thank you for all your grace and majesty unto me." Or, in a glorious affirmation of oneness, "You are everything to me, and I belong to you completely."

If I needed encouraging, I would be reminded, "Be happy and joyful in the Lord. Everything is coming through to you from Him. There is nothing to worry about." And I was constantly enjoined from within to "Go forward in the Light." This, I knew, meant to *live* the latihan.

Looking back over 1989 and 1990, it was clear that, for me, they had been years of questing and discovery, financed by the sale of my business interests. Certainly it had been a time of journeying, both inner and outer, including visits to Australia, Indonesia, Mexico and Portugal, and in September 1989 I had made my second trip to the United States, burning to 'tell the world' about the latihan and pursuing my belief that this was where my book should be published.

At that stage it was simply a story of spiritual crisis and recovery, albeit one that I sincerely believed merited publication as a personal account of the latihan in action. I was, however, somewhat daunted to discover that it would be far from easy to interest a mainstream publisher in a manuscript of this nature. But, as my receivings continued to deepen and multiply, they also began to suggest that my book was in any case far from complete: that it had a wider context than I was yet aware of and that it was but the beginning of a bigger story that I had yet to fully experience before it could be fully told.

You need not search any longer
to find God or the way to God.
The One who guides you and
leads you and enables you to
move and feel a vibration of
life within you *is* God.

Bapak
Los Angeles, June 1957
(67 LAX 2)

18

Intersection

One night towards the end of my second stay in America I received that something to do with Christ would shortly come about that would compel me to rewrite the beginning of my book. Soon afterwards, I was awakened by the word *Messiah*, coupled with an indication that something would somehow soon 'intersect' with my own experience to form a cross, and that this intersection would also show me how to write the ending.

Two weeks later I was moved to go to a local Catholic bookshop, where I was electrified to hear for the first time about the current apparitions of Mary the mother of Christ which had been occurring at Medjugorje in the former Yugoslavia, since June 24, 1981.

I was probably predisposed to be open to this phenomenon by the fact that both my parents had been miraculously cured of serious health challenges while visiting the Anglican Marian Shrine at Walsingham in England while I was a little boy. Nevertheless, despite this early influence, I had not grown up to be a practicing Christian, let alone a Catholic.

At the heart of the Medjugorje story are the thousands of appearances, continuing to this day, that, it is said, Mary has made to a small group of young villagers. These events have been accompanied and reinforced by hundreds of more general visitations and other supernatural events - similar to those which unfolded at Fatima, Portugal, in 1917 - which have been witnessed by many others, locals and visitors alike.

Comparing the messages attributed to Mary at Medjugorje with the transcripts of Bapak's many talks around the world, I was repeatedly struck by their similar content, often expressed in the very same words.

Both remind us that there is only one God, and both call for complete surrender to Him. In an interview recorded in January 1983, Mirjana, one of the young people to whom Mary had appeared, said, "She has always pointed out that there is only one God and that people have separated themselves. You cannot believe, you are not a Christian, if you do not respect other religions."

Like Bapak, and in company with all the sages from all the traditions across the centuries, the Virgin spoke of *opening the inner self* to the Lord, so suggestive of our latihan of inner surrender to the Most High.

In Mary's tireless reminders of the value of constant prayer "from the heart" and regular fasting, there was an unmistakable echo of Bapak's ceaseless encouragement to "stay close to the latihan" and to consider the need for *prihatin* (self-denial) and the annual fast of Lent or Ramadan.

Just as Bapak had urged Subud members to "live your latihan" so that God's grace would not be wasted, so Mary implored people to "live my messages" so that her mission and God's purpose will be fulfilled.

I was in fact stunned by the parallels between Mary's messages at Medjugorje and the words of Bapak, and by what I came to see as the relationship between Mary's call for a return to God and the dispensation of grace that is the latihan. I knew at once that this was the intersection I had been alerted to expect.

♦ ♦ ♦

Bapak had always discouraged proselytising, but I still found it extraordinary in this age of instant global communication that the existence and availability of the miracle of the latihan was completely unknown to the vast majority of the world's population. Clearly Bapak had envisaged that the time would come when there would be a dramatic increase in the number of people coming to Subud, but the fact remained that this grace was still contained within what one friend described as "the smallest spiritual movement in the world." This state of affairs contrasted markedly with Bapak's words in Washington D.C. in July 1981, when he said how great a mistake it would be if the latihan got "stuck with just a few people here and there." From the outset, my purpose in writing this book had stemmed from an instinctive feeling that it was now vital that the latihan should be brought to the attention of the world at large as a matter of urgency.

In my immediate reaction to the 'intersection' with Mary's message at Medjugorje, one aspect more than any other served to reinforce my original sense of urgent commitment in publishing my book. I am referring to the correlation I saw between Mary's warnings of pending global catastrophe and Bapak's occasional, more ambivalent allusions to this possibility. Combined with my own persistent and hitherto unshared receiving in this regard, it was this immediate recognition that also contributed to broadening my perception of where my book was heading (though I still had no idea as to its eventual destination), and imbued me with an even greater sense of responsibility and urgency towards getting it 'out there.'

That the world has never been in such peril was graphically restated by Our Lady at Medjugorje when she told one of the visionaries of a conversation between God and the devil. The devil maintained that people only believe in God when life is good; when things turn bad, he argued, people blame God or cease to believe in Him altogether. To put mankind to the test, Mary said, God had allowed the devil this one century in which to exercise an extended power over the world, exactly the same revelation received by Pope Leo XIII in his private chapel some one hundred years ago, at which time he was observed to be in great distress.

With just a few years of this satanic licence left to run, I did not feel it was unreasonable to assume that we are very close to what could well prove to be a cataclysmic settlement of accounts.

Much of my own receiving had certainly carried with it the implication that the world is heading for upheaval. During the Ramadan of 1990, for example, I received two clear indications in this connection. In the first, I was shown that there would be three days of global turmoil, the first of which would be the hardest to bear "because of the very strong winds that would blow." In the second, a dream, the winds had started to blow and I was trying to make others aware of the fact. It was shown to me that those who would not accept the meaning and reality of the winds were among those not destined to survive. Although this dream was frightening, it was not a nightmare. I awoke from it feeling calm, detached and strong. Much later, I came across a revelation of Our Lady delivered at Medjugorje on 15 February 1984 in which she said, "The wind is my sign. I will come in the wind. When the wind blows, know that I am with you. Do not be afraid."

Those who might be inclined to dismiss such utterances as religious clap-trap or superstitious mumbo-jumbo would do well to remember that Mary's very specific warnings at Fatima in

1917 of a second world war and of the error and repression that would spread from an atheistic Russia were in due course realised in full. (Later in this book we will look at the whole question of Fatima in rather more detail.)

One of my own crisis receivings had begun with the statement that "Nation shall rise against nation," and even as I was writing *Revelation Subud* (the original version of this book, published in 1991) the first conflict in the Persian Gulf was demonstrating once again just how quickly and easily our world can be brought to the edge of the abyss. Since then, the destruction of the Twin Towers, the second Iraq war and the ongoing chaos in Afghanistan have further fanned the flames of human discord and enmity. Such events also serve to remind us that for thousands of years the Middle East has been posited as the venue for Armageddon, the final struggle between the forces of good and evil. They also dovetail with Mary's warnings of a succession of disasters on the road to a fearful climax.

It is a matter of history that the appearances of Our Lady have often coincided with eras of spiritual darkness and physical danger. Her mission at such times has invariably been to warn, to comfort and to renew faith. But in the past, such manifestations have been relatively short-lived, sometimes limited to a single vision or perhaps to a few days or weeks. Never have they persisted for anything like the duration of her appearances at Medjugorje, and never with such sustained regularity or intensity.

In all her many manifestations in our time, Mary's warnings of Divine retribution have been coupled with a promise that the worst may yet be avoided if humanity will only turn back to God. The most specific indications that a spiritual clock is ticking were given by Mary to yet another group of simple village children in Garabandal, northern Spain, in the early 1960s.

In the middle of the night of 11 November 1987, I awoke to hear a loud voice, full of portent, say, "God is not yet ready to *stamp* His authority on man." I remembered this when I heard about the three momentous secrets Mary revealed at Garabandal.

19

Garabandal

Locations such as Lourdes and Fatima are virtually household names throughout the Christian world, even among non-Catholics. But Garabandal, a tiny village at the end of a single road that peters out in the Cantabrian Mountains of north-western Spain, is virtually unknown by comparison, perhaps in part because the drama that was enacted there in the early 1960s has not yet been officially recognized by the Catholic Church. It is, nevertheless, the launch pad for a spiritual time bomb that is destined to make it one of the most famous places on the planet. I spent a few days there in June 2005, enthralled by the timeless peace of this real life Shangri-la, palpably pregnant with the promise of great things to come.

Here, on 18 June 1961, the Archangel Michael appeared to four unsophisticated village girls, aged 11 and 12, signalling the start of what was to be a series of apparitions and extraordinary spiritual phenomena extending over four years. The angel told the children that he had come to prepare them for the visitation of the Blessed Virgin Mary, who would make her first appearance to them on Sunday, 2 July.

On that day, Mary duly appeared to the children in the first of hundreds of such manifestations, which were to continue until the final apparition on 13 November 1965. The girls described their visitor as a young woman aged about 18 wearing a white robe and a blue mantle. The encounters would last anything from a few minutes to several hours, and throughout each encounter the children would be in a trancelike state, staring ecstatically upwards, impervious to their surroundings. At such times, these otherwise entirely normal village youngsters would not react to any external stimulus, such as having bright lights shone in their eyes or their skin pricked with sharp pins. Many of these tests, along with the 'impossible' physical feats they were able to perform during the apparitions, were filmed and photographed.[1]

During the course of the Garabandal apparitions, Mary revealed three great secrets to her seers: prophecies of future happenings the likes of which the world has never seen.

The First Secret: On 1 January 1965, Our Lady told the young visionaries that God is going to send a supernatural **Warning** that will be seen and experienced by everyone everywhere. In the words of Conchita Gonzalez, one of the four, its outer form will be "like a crashing star, full of noise and light," and, although of itself it will not hurt anyone, it will be accompanied by a world-wide experience of conscience within every human being: in that moment, we will all see both the wrong we have done and the good we have failed to do.

The Second Secret: Our Lady went on to tell the children that within one year of the Warning God will send a great **Miracle**, an unprecedented event that will leave a mystical sign in the sky over Garabandal, one that people will be able to see but not touch, one that will endure for all time. Everyone who is present on this occasion will, according to the Virgin, be cured of whatever disease may afflict them.

---

[1] www.garabandal.org

The Third Secret: The purpose of the Warning and Miracle is to prove that God does exist and to highlight to the whole world just how far mankind has drifted from Him. If we do not heed these indications from Heaven, signs that every single human being will be witness to, and turn back to God, He will send the **Chastisement**, a punishment so dire that when Mary was telling the visionaries about it they were heard by the other villagers to be screaming in terror. In an interview years later for a BBC documentary, Conchita, herself now the mother of three children, said that the Chastisement is so terrible that if it comes "it would be better for my children if they had never been born."

Unprecedented though these prophecies are, they will be underscored and magnified by yet another unique dimension. Alone of the four visionaries, Conchita has been told the date of the Miracle. She has also been entrusted with a heavy responsibility, in that eight days before that date she is to announce its imminence to people everywhere. At that time, the date will be inserted in press releases that have already been prepared ready for distribution to the world's media, as a result of which the most stupendous spiritual phenomenon in history will be beamed to every corner of the globe as it unfolds

The more one looks for God, the
greater the distance one puts
between oneself and God.
The best way is simply to be still,
silent, conscious and at peace.
In that state, man will be able to
feel the contact with the Life
Force that envelops all worlds.

Bapak
San Francisco, March 1958
(58 SFO 1)

20

Pilgrimage

On the last morning of my second visit to the United States, I was collected from my San Diego hotel by a Subud friend I had got to know during my stay in Jakarta. As soon as he arrived, he told me of a clear dream he had had the night before in which the two of us stood together looking at my itinerary. An entry relating to Medjugorje[1] stood out from all the others.

As soon as I could arrange it, I was *en route* to Bosnia Herzegovina.

◆ ◆ ◆

It is difficult to imagine how Medjugorje must have appeared to the visitor before 1981, except by comparison with neighbouring hamlets, because the original character of the village has been totally eclipsed by the constant attention it receives from the outside world, especially during the summer. Scores of buses and taxis jam its streets, parked alongside dozens of look-alike souvenir shops, all competing for the foreign exchange of each day's quota of the thousands of visitors, whose English,

---

[1] http://www.medjugorje.net

Irish, American, German, French and Italian voices somehow meld in the lingua franca of their common purpose.

Yet none of this detracts from the immediate impression that something truly special, something deeply spiritual, is happening here. The church itself, set well back from the road, stands aloof from the commercialism as if to endorse this perception.

St. James' church, simple but impressive in design and superbly floodlit after dark, was crowded throughout my five day stay, as service succeeded service in all the languages necessary to minister to the multinational influx. A public address system relayed the proceedings to those outside. The large square surrounding the church was usually as crowded as the church itself, with impromptu groups praying together or listening to their own priest or guide; with dozens of people saying, or waiting for, confession in the open air; with individuals seeking solitude either on the benches provided or in the adjacent grassy areas.

As soon as I had found somewhere to stay, I dumped my suitcase and hurried to the church, where I immediately met Inge, a Danish pilgrim in her mid-sixties whom I had seen in a dream the night before. A recent convert to Catholicism, she was on her second visit to Medjugorje. Somehow our eyes met in mutual recognition, and we began to talk. She tried without success to describe the grace she had experienced on her previous visit, her tears of joy far more eloquent than her words.

Inge was able to give me a good impression of the local scene and, in particular, spoke with keen anticipation of Our Lady's monthly message. It seemed that, although Mary appears every day to the young seers and gives them a personal message, on the 25th of each month her message is a special one for the whole world and is posted in the church vestibule. By a happy coincidence, I had arrived in Medjugorje on the afternoon of Tuesday, October 24.

That evening I received a strong latihan, very loving and worshipful, and that night I had two clear dreams: one in which Bapak came very close to me, and another in which I was shown a cover design for my book.

◆ ◆ ◆

The following morning I walked up Krizevac Hill to the giant concrete cross that dominates the area, a place of miracles and apparitions. It was a gruelling climb up an extremely steep, rocky path, and is an important act of penance and sacrifice for many pilgrims. Some pray aloud as they climb, despite their shortness of breath, and not a few make the ascent barefoot.

The view from the top is breathtaking: in one direction overlooking a stunning panorama of Medjugorje and its environs, a carpet of intricate design spread far below, and in another revealing a mountain range that stretches into an ethereal infinity in folds of purple and blue – mystical, mysterious, and achingly beautiful.

Scattered across the summit are innumerable wooden crosses, brought from every point of the compass. I made my way to a quiet hollow, where I stood alone in a latihan of praise before falling to my knees in thanksgiving. Appropriately enough, in view of my own recent travels in America, the cross erected in that place had been carried overland across the U.S.

Back in the village for lunch, I relaxed in the warm sunshine reflecting on what I saw around me and looking forward to the posting of Mary's message later in the day.

By now, I confess that I had begun to find the non-stop broadcasting of services, particularly sermons, rather irksome. I felt that the practice seemed to allow little space for inner quietness, for the cultivation of 'that peace which the world cannot give.' Presumably most people are only here for a day or so and

often only for a few hours, I noted in my journal, and then return to the materialism and pressures of modern life. Is the
power of God really touching and changing many of these
people under these circumstances, I asked myself. Everyone is
sincerely reaching out here, but how many are making a real
inner contact? Outwardly, they are praying, praying, praying,
but where are they coming from, and are they really going
within?

I overheard one priest urging his flock to spend the whole day
on one prayer, concentrating on each individual word, one at a
time. Asking in my journal for protection from, and forgiveness
for, any misunderstanding on my part or tendency towards
spiritual pride, I wondered how this could possibly lead to the
inner prayer Our Lady is calling for.

I couldn't wait to get to the church that evening to read Mary's
message. I felt full of the latihan as I made my way across the
square, the inner prayer pulsing stronger than ever, "Father, Father, Father." The message is reproduced below. The italics are
mine.

> Dear children. Today also I am inviting you to prayer. I am
> always inviting you *but you are still far away*. Therefore, from
> today decide seriously to dedicate time to God. I am with
> you and I wish to teach you to pray with the heart. In
> prayer with the heart you shall encounter God. Therefore,
> little children, pray, pray, pray. Thank you for having re-
> sponded to my call.

If I had already caught occasional glimpses of what I saw as the
connection between Medjugorje and the latihan, it was this
message – and particularly those telling words *but you are still far
away* – that, for me at least, brought the correlation into sharp
focus.

At Medjugorje, Mary is calling for a profound human renewal, a deep and lasting change in the very hearts of people everywhere. She has been pleading for this transformation without a break since 1981, warning of a nemesis that will be upon us soon. As recently as April 2009 Mary told the visionary Mirjana[1]:

> God's love is in my words . . . the love which desires to turn you to justice and truth. That is the love which desires to save you from delusion. And what about you, my children? Your hearts remain closed; they are hard and do not respond to my call. They are insincere.

Mary is calling people to God. Calling, calling, calling. *But we are still far away; our hearts remain closed.*

With the latihan, God is making possible the response that Mary is urging, offering a spiritual door through which men and women everywhere may walk at this critical time.

The latihan is an *opening* to a living contact with His power: *bringing Him close.*

---

[1] To help you tune into the wonder of Medjugorje, I urge you to watch the video of this particular apparition as it unfolds. Go to http://crownofstars.blogspot.com and scroll a long way down to the April 18 posting. Click on the screen entitled 'Messaggio a Mirjana 2.4.09' immediately below the photo of the man painting a blue house. Keep your eyes on Mirjana's face as you watch the video and you will see the moment the Virgin appears to her – exactly as if she were suddenly moved into a deep latihan. It is an exquisite and intensely moving thing to witness.

This state of receiving has come
to man through the mercy of God,
and it is by His Grace that we are
able to receive the higher power
which is beyond our understanding
and thought processes.

Bapak
London, August 1959
(59 LON 5)

21

Revelation

The next day, Thursday, my third in Medjugorje, I seemed to drift through time and place, flowing from moment to moment without plan or intention. After lunch, to my surprise, I experienced a latihan of tears and heaviness, and then slept. I awoke still feeling full of sorrow and close to weeping. The feelings of aloneness and alienation from the throng around me had never been stronger.

I then realized that my sadness was due to a renewed awareness of my smallness compared to the greatness of Almighty God — something of a throwback to my crisis state. By evening, my spiritual self was able to worship God in a very beautiful latihan: "He is everything. All praise and worship be to Him. From Him alone can come whatever may be needed. God be praised and worshipped above all."

From past experience I knew that this total surrender, this reminder of my complete dependence upon God, could well be a prelude to an important receiving.

In the morning I was awakened by a vision of Christ.

I received instantly and completely that my book should be
Christ-centered and should bear witness to the truth that

THE LATIHAN
IS A
MANIFESTATION
OF THE
SECOND COMING.

22

Perfect Love

I still had a day and a half to spend in Medjugorje, and by now I was looking forward to returning to the five-star luxury of my Dubrovnik hotel. I drifted through Friday, impatient to be on my way, and spent the first part of Saturday morning in much the same way until around 11 o'clock, when I started back to my room to pack for a 3 p.m. departure.

Along the way, I chanced upon a group of pilgrims gathered to listen to Mirjana, one of the original child visionaries and now a beautiful young woman in her early twenties who works for a local travel agency. I had a shorthand pad with me and was able to take verbatim notes of what was said. She began by apologising for the fact that she had very little free time from her job that day, and, speaking through an interpreter, she then made a short opening statement before inviting questions from her audience.

> Mirjana: Our Lady regards everyone the same, those who go to church and those who do not. She regards herself as the mother of all, those who are close to God and those who are not.

Question: Did Our Lady mention anything about the Eastern religions?

Mirjana: She said that we are all her children, all people. We ourselves made religions, we divided our selves.

Question: What does Our Lady mean by conversion? From atheism to Christianity? From other branches of Christianity to Catholiscism? Or what?

Mirjana: Conversion actually means to turn your back on sin and walk towards God. It does not mean leaving one denomination and transferring to another. Start praying with the heart, walking closer and closer to God the Father.

The remaining questions concerned such areas of general interest as Our Lady's actual appearance, and the short exchange was soon over. It was around noon when I sat down to make the following note in my journal: 'I was getting quite uncomfortable here among all these intense people, what with the constant services and prayer by rote. How beautiful to round off my visit by seeing and hearing Mirjana. She is so open, simple and relaxed, so Subud-like somehow. Afterwards, there was a tangible, other-worldly quality and beauty in the air, and even now I am moved to tears of love and sweetness.'

I am not entirely sure what happened next. I remember getting to my feet to resume my walk back to my room when I was suddenly and completely overwhelmed by a pure love that defies description. I ran blindly into the field next to the church where I sobbed without restraint in a condition of utter abandonment before Almighty God. I was totally possessed by a love that caused something in my chest to melt. It was like being given the Subud contact for the second time, but in a new way. *This love was everything.*

I prostrated myself in joy and worship as the latihan coursed through me – "Maria, Christus, *Allah 'u Akbar* (God is Great) – its boundless grace merging with the mystery of Medjugorje.

There was no longer any separation between the two. I was at one with all creation, and I *knew* that God is love. The intersection was complete. My tears fell on the grass of Medjugorje, and this perfect love flowed out to all around me.

I stood as the latihan poured through me: "Praise the Lord, O my soul. All that is within me bless His holy name."

Whereupon, from my ordinary heart, transformed: *How can I bear to leave this special place and all these dear people?* And the inner reply, "The Lord is with you."

Then, through the sweet tears of this almost unbearable love, I was moved anew from within to pledge total service to God and to promise to follow wherever He might lead.

Subud is not a religion, but a receiving
that arises from beyond the influence
and effort of the heart and mind. This
receiving can be described as simply
the practice of what is hoped for and
looked for by the religions and what
is looked for outside of religion.

Bapak
Woodstock, June 1981
(81 WOS 1)

23

Corroboration

In May 1990 I travelled to the United States for the third time, once again following my guidance that this was where *Revelation Subud* (the title of the first version of this book) should initially be published. Medjugorje had indeed proved to be the 'intersection' I had been guided to expect, and at that point I felt that it had also shown me how it should end. I was eager to press on with the final editing of my manuscript, but in fact this was not yet to be.

During the early hours of my first night back in America, I awoke to find myself confronting an apparition of Our Lady. She appeared to me in outline only, just as (I later discovered) she had first appeared to one of the child visionaries at Medjugorje. I sat up and she advanced to my bedside. Like the sweetest of mothers, she gently placed her fingers over my mouth as if to silence me and said, "Your book won't come out yet." Then she paused before going on to confirm the rightness of my being in America: "You have begun to sing with new Subud friends. And I approve of this."

I was intensely disappointed that yet again it seemed I must put my book aside. Although very moved by the visitation, I felt completely thrown by Mary's intervention, and it took me at least a week to recover an attitude of acceptance and patience. It seemed obvious that the significance of Mary's remark related to the timing of the project, and, following my guidance and testing, I remained in the U.S. and began to work with a few small, struggling Subud business enterprises.

This was in harmony both with the second part of Mary's message and also with Sudarto's comment about enterprises that had seemed so out of context when I had met with him in Jakarta.

Following one's spiritual guidance is not always easy; it is sometimes open to misinterpretation on the ordinary level and does not always bestow instant understanding of its full meaning or purpose. It calls for faith and courage – especially when one feels one has none! – and even a willingness to make mistakes. For the past few years I had been called upon to try and live such a life, often unsure of my direction and destination, but always seeking to 'go forward in the light.' It wasn't until several months after my experiences in Medjugorje that I began to feel that everything was falling into place; that, by the grace and will of an all-merciful God, I could see His way for me a little more clearly.

When I had been deeply in crisis, well over a year before I had the first impulse to write this book, the figure of Christ had suddenly appeared in front of me during latihan. "I will write the foreword to your book," he said to me. He then paused and fixed with me a long, piercing look. "And that means," he continued, referring to the book, "that it will be big." At the time, this meant absolutely nothing to me, and I virtually forgot about it. With *Revelation Subud* nearing completion, however, I would remember this experience from time to time and wonder about my book's missing foreword.

Reflecting upon this experience today, some twenty years later, I find myself wondering whether "writing the foreword" might in fact have referred to the long process of preparation and experience that would be necessary before this final version could see the light of day. Back in 1990, however, a month after I had seen the apparition of Mary, I was thrilled to come across a little-known quotation by Bapak which, I felt, dovetailed perfectly with my receiving at Medjugorje, and which, prompted by a clear dream, I adopted as the foreword of *Revelation Subud* and have repeated in the penultimate chapter of this book.

When you were a newborn baby
your connection with your soul
was still close.
Gradually, you got to know the
world but forgot your soul.
That is why receiving and feeling
the latihan seems like something
new, whereas in fact it is not.
This latihan has been available
ever since human beings were
born in this world.

Bapak
Los Angeles, June 1967
(67 LAX 2)

24

With One Voice

I happen to believe that we who have been so blessed as to receive this priceless gift we call the latihan are potentially uniquely equipped to tune into the universality of the spiritual truth personified in the likes of Jesus Christ and the Prophet Muhammad — to say nothing of Bapak himself; and that we can do this without falling prey to the disunity and conflict that so often goes along with a rigid adherence to the narrow limitations of belief that over the centuries have come to characterise aspects of many of the great religions.

In the earliest days of Islam, acting on the advice of Muhammad himself, the very first Muslim emigrants escaped persecution in Mecca by travelling to Christian Abyssinia, where they were well received. The Negus (supreme ruler) of that country asked if they had with them any revelation that their prophet had received from God, whereupon Ja'far, their spokesman, recited a passage from Koran (the sura — chapter - of Mary), which had been revealed shortly before their departure:

> And make mention of Mary in the Book, when she withdrew from her people unto a place towards the east, and secluded herself from them; and We sent unto her Our Spirit, and it appeared to her in the likeness of a perfect man. She said, I take refuge from thee in the Infinitely

Good, if any piety thou hast. He said: I am none other than a messenger from thy Lord, that I may bestow on thee a son most pure. She said: How can there be for me a son, when no man hath touched me, nor am I unchaste? He said: Even so shall it be; thy Lord sayeth: It is easy for Me. That We may make him a sign for mankind and a mercy from Us; and it is a thing ordained.[1]

Both the ruler and his bishops were moved to tears as they listened, and the Negus said, "This hath truly come from the same source as that which Jesus brought."

Unexpectedly to some perhaps, the Oneness underlying the spiritual reality at the heart of the great faiths of Christianity and Islam – and by extension Judaism, Hinduism and Buddhism, etc. – was attested to by Mary during an apparition at Medjugorje. At one point, the visionaries asked her to nominate someone in the community who could be said to be a fine, God-fearing exemplar. Our Lady obliged by singling out Pasha, a woman of Sarajevo, a former neighbour of one of the visionaries. "But she's a Muslim," protested the children. "She is a true believer, a saintly woman. You should try to be more like her," was Mary's response.

This same breadth of vision can also be discerned in the sayings of the Prophet of Islam. "Satan toucheth every child of Adam the day his mother beareth him," he said, "save only Mary and her son."[2] Muhammad also predicted the coming of the Antichrist, who would cause great corruption on earth in the latter days. And he prophesied the Second Coming of Christ, adding "And the enemy of God, when he see-eth Jesus, will melt even

---

[1] Koran XIX, 16-21

[2] Muhammad ibn Isma'il al-Bukhari LX, 54

as salt melteth in water. If he were let be, he would melt unto perishing; but God will slay him at the hand of Jesus."[1]

The Prophet also foresaw the ultimate unity of Islam and Christianity: "God," he said, "will bring us together," thereby echoing Mary's words at Medjugorje: "There is only One God, one Faith. Muslims, Orthodox and Catholics to my Son and myself are all one. You are all my children."

One of my own experiences, I feel, testified to Mary's dynamic barrier-bridging role in today's world. It took the form of a clear dream in which I had had a breakthrough in my work and, energized by the power of God, I was on my way to give a talk. I was carrying the text of my speech with me and happened to bump into a group of Catholic cardinals. "You think too much!" I said to them and at the same time one of the pieces of paper I was holding dropped to the ground. One of the cardinals bent to retrieve it for me and saw that it was headed with Mary's seal. He looked at me in amazement. "Mary?" he said. "Who else?" I replied.

Mary's unique unifying role was recognized in 1980 – just one year before the first of the apparitions at Medjugorje – by the Sufi Shaikh Conya-Sulaiman-Dad when he said, "The Virgin Mary is the only one who can build a bridge between true Muslims and true Christians, and she will indeed come to offer to do this very soon." A key word here, I would suggest, is 'true.'

This had been precisely the indication received by John Bennett some 20 years earlier. In 1959, Bennett, a key figure in facilitating the spread of Subud during Bapak's first visit to the West, was invited to visit the Benedictine Monastery of St. Wandrille in northern France. After giving explanations about

---

[1] Muslim ibn al-Hajjaj al-Qushayri LII, 9

the latihan, he passed on the contact to three of the fathers, one of whom became the next abbot.[1]

In his autobiography *Witness,* Bennett wrote:

> During my stay in the monastery I received several illuminating experiences in the latihan. Once I heard a voice within me saying, "Surrender to the will of God is the foundation of all religion." Then I became aware of the presence of Jesus and saw that he is the manifestation of the Love of God.
>
> The thought entered my mind, "Then Christianity is the one true religion." At the same moment I found myself intoning the opening chapter of the Koran. ("Glory to God, the Lord of the worlds, the Compassionate, the Merciful.")
>
> Then the same voice said, "It is my will that my Church and Islam should be united." I said in astonishment, "Who could accomplish such a task?" And the reply came, "Mary."

It so happens that Mary is mentioned thirty times in the Koran, more times than in the Bible. No other woman is mentioned at all in Islam's holy book. She is in fact one of only eight people to have a chapter named after her, and, according to two early sources,[2] the Prophet Muhammad allowed a picture of an icon of the Virgin Mary and the child Jesus to be one of only two paintings to remain within the precincts of the Ka'aba itself, Islam's holy of holies in Mecca, the other being a painting of the Prophet Abraham.

Our Lady's potentially unifying role was strikingly evident in a series of apparitions from 1968 through 1971, during which period she appeared almost nightly, often for hours at a time,

---

[1] This man, the Reverend Albert-Jacques Bescond, later contributed to a Subud periodical, extracts from which are included at Appendix A.

[2] Muhammad ibn 'Umar al-Waqidi (834) and Muhammad ibn 'Abd Allah al-Azraqui (1, 107)

above the Coptic Orthodox Church of St. Mary at Zeitoun, Cairo, as well as above a local mosque.[1] During these three years, she was seen by 1,500,000 people, mostly Muslims. The apparitions were broadcast on Egyptian TV, photographed by hundreds of professional photographers and personally witnessed by the then President, Abdul Nasser. It is reported that every night she "maintained a wondrous silence" and an attitude of prayer to Almighty God. In this way, it was recognised, she ensured a unanimity of reverence and prayerfulness on the part of all present, regardless of their religious differences.

These 'differences' have no place in the realm of the human soul, and in the latihan they vanish like the morning dew in the warmth of the sun. In the latihan, just as expressed in the words of one witness to the Zeitoun miracle, "There were Muslims and Christians, and everyone was as one, one religion together." Indeed, given that the full meaning of Islam is 'to achieve wholeness by surrendering one's will and committing it entirely to the safekeeping of the One Almighty God' and given that there can be no greater benchmark of this ideal than Jesus, who would not yearn to be both a true Muslim *and* a true Christian?!

I love the way Bapak expressed the same sentiment during a talk in Santiago de Chile in May 1967:

Take Bapak: he is not a member of the Christian religion, but he is Christian. As for Islam, that is clear, because he is a Muslim. If you are quiet, truly quiet, all you feel is God: 'God is great; God.' You should feel it like this. [*Bapak demonstrates by moving his body from side to side and backward and forward.*]

---

[1] http://www.zeitun-eg.org/stmaridx.htm

It is a cross. It means that Bapak carries a cross within him. But not a picture of a cross. No. Not a cross made of silver or steel. No. It is an inner cross. It is alive.

I recall him on another occasion speaking in similar vein of the Koran, saying that the true Koran was a *living* reality inside him.

Prophet Muhammad also bore witness to the sovereignty of Spirit over letter: *If all the trees in the earth were pens, and if the sea eked out by seven seas more were ink, the Words of God could not be written out unto their end.* [1]

---

[1] Koran XXXXI, 27

25

A Pause for Breath

I self-published much of this book in the United States in mid-1991 under the title *Revelation Subud*. The book sold well to Subud members all over the world. Also, by virtue of a highly positive review in the American *Library Journal* it was bought by public libraries the length and breadth of the United States. In addition to that, the book was picked up by a leading New Age distributor in America, which generated a significant nation-wide boost to my personal sales efforts calling on bookstores in and around Los Angeles, where I lived at the time.

After a few months, I received an unexpected offer of publication in the U.K. from the proprietor of what I assumed was a successful, well-established publishing company. Because of this I set aside my own amateur marketing endeavours in America to return to England. I was eager to have my book produced by a 'proper' publisher, as well as to use the opportunity to round off my story in the light of new experiences and important new information. Unfortunately, the publishing enterprise involved was not as solid as I had thought and it folded within a month or so of publishing *Latihan,* the successor to *Revelation Subud.* For better or worse, my involvement with this company brought my own self-publishing momentum to a standstill and it never recovered. Nevertheless, I was glad of the chance represented by the second edition to acknowledge and address the disquiet expressed by those Subud members for whom the first edition of my book had proved to be quite controversial.

On the one hand, it had precipitated a wealth of heart-warming feedback from many who were touched and helped by what they recognised as an honest sharing of experience. Some of these people were delighted to see Subud being given more of a Christian slant than what, in the early days, they considered to be an overly Islamic orientation. But there were also expressions of concern from a few people of diverse backgrounds who feared that my presentation of its action within *me* would misrepresent both the universality and the individuality of the exercise. In short, they feared that my book was *too* Christian!

For my part, when at Medjugorje I received that the latihan is 'a manifestation of the Second Coming,' it came from a high spiritual source. Because of its origin, neither then nor since has it occurred to me to regard this revelation as either religious or even Christian in any rigid or fundamentalist sense. Like the latihan itself it never felt divisive. It was simply a spiritual reality.

Even my experiences of Jesus and Mary did not have a 'Christian' connotation; they were not wearing labels or clothed in the garments of separatism. The same could be said of the encounter with Prophet Muhammad, described herein, which was in fact one of three interactions I had with him. It was as if I were catching mere glimpses of beings of vast spiritual stature, whose God-given roles both nourish and transcend what we on earth call religion and who far outreach the puny understanding and rigid man-made divisions of our ordinary hearts and minds.

Then there were those – longstanding Subud members some of them – who were worried that my experiences would strike the average reader as quite simply unbelievable: the product, perhaps, of an over-active imagination, spiritual delusion or mental aberration. Yet others were afraid that potential Subud members would hope and expect that they too would soon receive the kind of experiences that were visited upon me, albeit after more than 30 years of latihan.

Their anxiety moved me to stress that the latihan is a unique experience for each person, that extreme patience is often called for before one even begins to be aware of its action and that crisis experiences in particular are decidedly not normal, are in fact also quite rare and certainly not to be sought after for their own sake. At such a time, a person is in a heightened state of spiritual awareness, is unusually open and much closer than usual to the reality of Almighty God. In such a state, a person is often unable to function normally for an extended period of time.

A concern of my own was that the sheer severity of my purification process would have the very opposite effect than the one I hoped for: that, instead of encouraging people to want to receive the latihan for themselves, my story might actually deter them from doing so. This remains my concern today, so, in addition to reminding the reader that what I went through is exceptional, I would also emphasise that it was the anxious response of my innate 'lack of courage' that both prolonged and exacerbated the entire process.

Nevertheless, I was thrilled from time to time to hear of people who did come to Subud as a result of reading the first edition of my book and to hear of two people who received the contact spontaneously while reading it.

My feeling is that those who decide to follow through on this memoir and ask to receive the contact will be among the more serious seekers, those who are truly ready for it, those who are sincerely prepared to surrender themselves to the greatness that we call God.

Wherever it might lead, I just *knew* that I had to write the book and when I returned home from delivering the original manuscript to the typesetter, I had barely walked through the door before I was overwhelmed with an experience of God's love almost as powerful as at Medjugorje. Once again, I could barely contain it and all I could do was cry out, "I just don't know what to do with this love." After a while the intensity of the experience diminished and I received, "You have my complete support and blessing."

A year later, in 1992, with the publication of *Latihan* — something of a damp squib compared to the relative success of *Revelation Subud* — I was able to bring my story up to date with an account of a meeting which seemed to go a long way towards clarifying the nature of my crisis.

26

A Remarkable Meeting

During the final weeks of editing *Revelation Subud* I received a telephone call from Mark (Erling) Week, a longstanding Subud member of whom I had heard but never met. It seems that he had heard something of my experiences from Simon Sturton, a mutual friend in England, and the purpose of the call was to suggest a meeting.

At this stage I was living in Los Angeles and, as luck would have it, Mark and Istimah Week had recently moved to the San Diego area, about one hundred miles south. We arranged a meeting and the timing worked out perfectly; I was able to mail my typeset manuscript to the printers the very day before I drove south.

Meeting the Weeks was a delight. Since my crisis I had been extremely sensitive to the inner content of people near me, and with both Mark and Istimah it was a joy to tune in to their exceptionally fine inner natures.[1]

---

[1] Mark died on 8 September 2006, aged 91, and Istimah on 13 November 2008, aged 85.

Almost immediately we sat down to lunch, and we passed a pleasant hour exchanging news and reminiscences of mutual friends around the world. It was only after the meal, while we were strolling together in the sunshine near his home, that Mark brought up the subject that had prompted his phone call. Before long, I realized that there was much more to this meeting than a merely pleasant encounter.

"I think you should know," Mark began, "about an experience I had during a latihan in Jakarta in 1968. I was standing on a hill looking up at the sky and in the sky was the earth, twice the size of the moon. I realized that everyone in the world was also outside, looking at the sky and seeing this impossible thing. Then a very bright source of light shone down, hitting the earth at different points on the different continents.

"A year later in a meeting with perhaps fifty other helpers, I had occasion to tell Bapak about this experience, and he asked, 'How many rays of light were there?' Immediately after the experience I had realized the importance of this question and had decided that there were more than twelve and less than fifty, which I now put to Bapak. He immediately responded, 'More than thirty and less than forty.'"

As Mark reached this point in his story I began to be aware of a strong vibration of the latihan within me. I remembered the light from space that had entered me in October 1986 at the beginning of my crisis, and I felt that I was hearing something of supreme importance to me personally.

I also remembered a clear crisis dream in which I saw myself walking shoulder to shoulder with an older man, rugged and powerful. "Do you know who this is?" asked a voice. "No," I replied. "That is a pity," continued the voice, "because this is one of the most caring people ever to walk on earth." Now, striding out side by side with Mark, I felt a sudden insight that he might be the mysterious older man.

"During the next stage of the experience," continued Mark, "I found myself walking into a big park in which there was a research building, a rambling construction that had obviously been built without an advance plan. There were Subud people walking around, and as I went up on to the verandah I realized that it was a Subud building, that in fact the building symbolised Subud itself.

"I looked through the window at one end of the building, into a room which I could see contained nothing but the statue of a Javanese dancer. I knew that this was a statue of Bapak, that Bapak was dead, and that the statue symbolised the first phase of Subud.

"I then looked into the adjoining room and saw a computer there about the size of a steamer trunk. In spite of its small size, however, I knew that it had a greater capacity than any other computer on earth and that it represented the second phase of Subud."

I could no longer contain myself: "The light from space, the computer – these are things that happened to me during my crisis," I said.

"I haven't finished yet," smiled Mark. "As the experience continued, it occurred to me that by looking at the manufacturer's plate on the computer I would be able to see when all this was going to happen. So I entered the second room and found a brass plate on the side of the computer. It bore the date 1987 – the year, of course, in which Bapak died.

"As I looked at the brass plate," continued Mark, "the date changed like a tachometer: 1988, 1989, 1990, 1991. Then it stopped, and Bapak confirmed that this is something that would really happen. 'In about twenty years time,' he said, 'between thirty and forty *rohani* souls [souls completely surrendered to the will of God] will come into the world, and after that nobody in the world will be able to say that God does not exist.'

"Bapak also asked me if I understood anything more about the computer, and I had to answer 'No' said Mark. But within a very short time I began to receive more understanding about it. I came to see that all the people who will possess, or be possessed by, the *rohani* force will be connected to the computer, so that if any one of them is asked a question he or she will be able in effect to call up an answer from the 'one great computer' and that the answer will be the same, no matter which of the *rohanis* is asked the question."

I listened intently to Mark's account, all too aware of the parallels between his vision of 1968 and my own computer/new brain experience of 1987.

And, although Mark couldn't know it, 1991 held almost as much significance for me as 1987. In the crisis dream in which I had seen myself being driven to my own funeral beneath a banner displaying the words, 'Complete Trust and Confidence,' I had been 55 years old, the age that I would reach in October 1991. Ever since that experience, I had been sure that in late 1991 either I would die or the process that had begun in me during my crisis would begin to bear fruit. In the event, this was the year when my first attempts to 'tell the world about Subud' *(Revelation Subud* and *Latihan)* were published.

♦ ♦ ♦

Despite the dramatic nature of much of what Mark had told me, I felt calm and peaceful as I drove back to L.A. after taking my leave of the Weeks. I had had to endure so much during and since my spiritual crisis, that again and again I had doubted my capacity to bear it; again and again I had wondered if I were losing my mind. Now, for the first time, I felt that I had been given some real insight into what had happened to me.

Soon afterwards I visited Mark and Istimah again, and we discussed a subject about which I had been deliberately less than forthright in *Revelation Subud*. Once again, the Weeks turned out to be a missing link, this time in relation to what has become known as the Third Secret of Fatima.

It is this connection you will need
when you come to the end of your life,
so that you will be guided.
The boundary then between life
and death will disappear.
It will simply be a transition
from not being to being.
You will then find that in the *not being*
you *are*.

Bapak
Melbourne, February 1978
(78 MEB 2)

27

The Secret of Fatima, Part I

On 13 October 1917, near the tiny village of Fatima in central Portugal, between seventy and one hundred thousand people witnessed an 'impossible' happening, a phenomenon that is as well documented in the literature and media of the time as any event in recorded history.[1]

Variously motivated by piety and hope, by incredulity and derision, the multitude had been drawn to this remote and unlikely region from all over the country. On this day, according to three simple village children, the beautiful Lady who had been appearing and speaking to them for the past six months would demonstrate the truth of her existence and of her message with a miracle, a supernatural sign that *everyone* – not just the three little seers – would see. What followed filled every heart with terror before transmuting hope into joy and unbelief into conviction.

To everyone's amazement, the sun suddenly began to glow and fade, throwing shafts of light first one way and then another. Astonishingly, everyone could look directly at the sun with ease

---

[1] http://www.fatima.org

as they observed it painting both themselves and their surroundings in all the colours of the rainbow.

After a while the display of light and colour came to an end,
giving way to an even more unbelievable spectacle: the sun began to tremble and dance and then seemed to loosen itself from
the sky. Then, in a terrible moment of suspense, it appeared to
hurl itself towards earth in a mighty zigzag motion, falling towards the crowd like a revolving ball of fire.

The mass of people were stricken with fear. Many fell to their
knees, begging for mercy, convinced that they were about to
die in what must surely be the end of the world. At the last
moment the sun swung back to its place in the heavens.

The promised miracle had taken place, confounding ridicule
and skepticism and setting the seal in no uncertain fashion
upon the apparitions of Our Lady of Fatima.

They had begun exactly six months earlier, on 13 May 1917,
when the three young shepherds – Lucia, Francisco and Jacinta
aged 10, 9 and 7 – experienced the first of six encounters with
a lady 'dressed all in white, more brilliant than the sun.'

Throughout the course of the apparitions, Our Lady of the
Rosary – for so she finally identified herself to the three children – urged prayer and self-sacrifice on behalf of peace in the
world and for a speedy end to the First World War.

During the apparition of 13 July, Our Lady gave the children a
message that was not to be revealed to anyone else at that time.
Within two years, as Mary had foreseen, Francisco and Jacinta
died, victims of the Spanish flu pandemic that swept across the
world after World War I, leaving Lucia as the sole custodian of a
four-part prophecy.

The surviving visionary went on to become a nun, and in 1927, reportedly in obedience to a direct instruction from Jesus, Sister Lucia divulged parts one, two and four of Our Lady's message. At this point, the third part was to remain a secret.

Thus it was learned that Mary had warned of a rain of retribution that would be visited upon humanity for the offences against Heaven caused by man's Godless ways: chastisements that would include the Second World War, the rise of Communism, the annihilation of several entire nations, the persecution of the faithful and the sufferings that would be visited upon the Pope. "In the end," Our Lady concluded in part four of the message, "My Immaculate Heart will triumph ... and a period of peace will be granted to the world."

In October 1930 the apparitions were officially recognized by the Catholic Church.

In 1943, Lucia – by this time a member of the convent of the Dorothean Sisters of Tuy in Spain – fell gravely ill and, fearing that she would die without revealing what had become known as the Secret of Fatima, the Bishop of Leiria visited the seer and asked her to write it down. She agreed to do so only if given a formal written instruction, and this was duly forthcoming. For three months, however, Sister Lucia could not comply with the request, finding herself impeded by a strange and fearful anguish whenever she tried to do so. This was later interpreted as a manifestation of diabolical obstruction, which persisted until 2 January 1944. On this day Our Lady reportedly appeared again to the nun, confirmed that it was truly in accordance with the will of God that the Secret be written down and imbued her with the strength to do so.

The Secret was placed in a sealed envelope and kept in the palace of the Bishop of Leiria until its eventual transfer to Rome thirteen years later. When the envelope was held up against a light, the Secret was seen to consist of between 20 and 25 words, written on a single sheet of paper.

It reached the office of Pope Pius XII on 16 April 1957, accompanied by an instruction from Mary to the effect that the Secret should be disclosed to the world in 1960 or upon Lucia's death, *whichever happened first.* In other words, it was clearly the will of God that the Secret should be made known by 1960 at the latest.[1] The visionary died in 2005, aged 97.

Surprisingly perhaps, when the envelope was passed to Pope John XXIII in 1959, one year after the death of Pius XII, it was found to be still sealed. It seems almost certain, therefore, that Pius XII had not read the Secret, for which no reasonable explanation has been offered. It would seem to be scarcely conceivable that this Pope, whose Papal Bull of 1950 promulgated the new dogma of the Assumption of the Blessed Virgin Mary, would be so disinterested in her message at Fatima as not to avail himself of his rightful access to it.

It is, however, well established that Popes John XXIII, Paul VI, John Paul II and Benedict XVI all read the Secret.

As 1959 drew to a close, a spirit of great anticipation gathered momentum within the Church as Catholics everywhere looked forward with eagerness to the disclosure of the mysterious third part of the message of Fatima. On 8 February 1960, this confident expectation was abruptly shattered by the low-key release via a Portuguese press agency of an anonymous Vatican communiqué stating that the secret would not be published, *and probably never would be.*

Astonishingly, in view of the fact that the Church had long since officially recognized the authenticity of the Fatima appa-

---

[1] *The Whole Truth about Fatima* by Brother Michael of the Holy Trinity C.R.C. (Buffalo, N.Y. and Fort Erie, Ontario: Immaculate Heart Publications), 1990.

ritions, the press release concluded: 'The Church does not desire to take the responsibility for guaranteeing the veracity of
the words the three shepherd children said that the Virgin Mary
had addressed to them.' This despite the fact that it had been
Mary's express wish that the secret be released to the world by
1960 at the latest – a time when, according to Sister Lucia herself, the message would appear "more clear."

◆ ◆ ◆

It so happens that at the very time the Catholic world was in a
state of high expectation, keenly awaiting the disclosure of the
Third Secret of Fatima, the West was in the earliest stage of becoming aware of the existence of the Subud latihan.

In the wake of the spiritual whirlwind that accompanied Bapak's first journey outside Indonesia in 1957, 1960 was a heady
time for the hundreds of new Subud members scattered around
the globe who knew that something momentous was happening. Half expecting that millions more would soon get to hear
about and respond to the reality of the latihan, we would not
have been surprised if the whole world had been changed
within a few years.

But 1960 came and went and neither of these two eventualities
was realised. The world at large did not get to hear about either
the newly available direct contact with the Holy Spirit or about
the Third Secret of Fatima: on the one hand, because Bapak
insisted that Subud should not be advertised, and, on the other,
because the Vatican chose not to reveal the long-awaited third
part of the Fatima message. Given what I know now, I cannot
help but do more than merely reflect upon the relative timing
of these two spiritual phenomena and upon their significance
and potential at a time when humanity was yearning for spiritual renewal and the West was instinctively looking towards the
East.

Inevitably, the Church's manifest determination not to release the Secret – some might say to thwart the will of Heaven – gave rise to the intense speculation that continues to this day among both Catholics and non-Catholics, despite, or maybe in part because of, the questionable version made public on 26 June, 2000 (see page 151).

It is not for me to presume to say categorically what is contained in the Secret of Fatima. Despite feeling driven from within to pursue this question, therefore, I have not approached it lightly and I was cautious about advancing the new evidence and information that came to my attention. On no less than three separate occasions, each time from a different standpoint, I sought guidance with others about the rightness of seeking to cast new light upon this aspect of the message delivered at Fatima. Each time the receiving was unanimously positive. I myself received that this was "my duty to God and to man." It was also during this period of doubt and self-questioning, in the profound quiet at the end of a particularly powerful latihan, that I found myself declaring, "There is absolutely no purpose in my being on earth other than to do Your will. If I cannot do that I should die." I then remembered a very clear dream of a few months earlier that had meant little to me at a time when *Revelation Subud* (the forerunner of this book) was already in production and, seemingly, my opportunity to address the Fatima question had passed.

In the dream I was about to climb into a scaled-down version of the 'Popemobile.' Ahead of me stretched a broad highway with a slightly downward incline. There was no other traffic on the road and nothing else that might hinder my progress. Waiting for me at the bottom of the slope was His Holiness Pope John Paul II, smiling encouragingly. He stood in front of a road sign, just like a traffic policeman, beckoning me forward and indicating that I should turn to my left. The sign also pointed in that direction, and when I looked at the words on it I saw that they read 'The Secret of Fatima.'

Although not a Catholic, it is nevertheless with the greatest respect and sympathy for the predicament in which the Church might well have found itself, therefore, that I use the word 'questionable' to describe the version of the Secret released by the Vatican in June 2000.

My reasons for doing so are threefold:

Firstly, the lack of correlation between the content of the published text and Lucia's own statement that by 1960 the meaning of the message would appear "more clear."

Secondly, the significance of Pope John Paul II's response to renewed pressure from the Italian media in the mid-eighties, when he said that he did not wish to "encourage false prophets" by revealing the Secret.

And thirdly, Bapak's own contribution to the debate, made during a conversation with Mark and Istimah Week in 1968.

Before elaborating on all this, I must first return to my personal story and to an account of my second meeting with Mark and Istimah.

> **When one is able to know one's inner self, it's the same as knowing God.**
>
> *Bapak*
> *The Hague, September 1957*
> *(57 HAG 3)*

28

The Secret of Fatima, Part II

For decades it had been strongly rumoured within the Subud community that the Secret of Fatima was in some way linked to the coming of the latihan. I had been very tempted to refer to this in *Revelation Subud*. At that time, however, my knowledge was limited to vague hearsay, and I did not wish to diminish the credibility of my own experience and receiving by engaging in unsubstantiated speculation.

During my second meeting with Mark and Istimah, however, I realised that I had come face to face with two first-hand witnesses who were in a unique position to contribute vital, complementary evidence, witnesses whose integrity I have every reason to respect and whose testimony should, I believe, be heard by all those with a sincere, open-minded interest in the relevance and purpose of Our Lady's messages at Fatima and since then, with increasing frequency and urgency, elsewhere.

Mark Week had been accustomed to powerful spiritual manifestations from his youth. From the age of twelve, during long nights in prayer, he began to experience feelings of bliss entering through the top of his head, sometimes accompanied by ideas that did not arise from himself. At the same time, he also embarked upon a seven year period of what Bapak would have called *prihatin* (self-denial), with the objective of overcoming feelings of anger, dislike and fear, and of detaching himself from everything and everyone.

In 1934, when he was a nineteen-year-old honours student at the University College of California at Berkeley, Mark underwent an experience of special significance in which he suddenly found himself in a place 'before the beginning': a place in which his perception of himself was that of being a dimensionless point possessed of consciousness. There was no space, no time, no body, no senses and no 'other.'

As he began to return from that place, Mark said, his first experience of 'other' was of being surrounded in all directions by points of 'being' in the darkness — all, like himself, sending out vibrations. Some had a harmonic rhythm and felt very nice, while others had a disharmonious rhythm and felt painful. He then entered a state of contemplative consciousness, a state beyond the action of the thinking mind that he later recognized as what St. John of the Cross had described as 'infused contemplation,' and which later still he would experience in the latihan as clear receiving.

"In this state," Mark explained, "I was given to understand that the vibrating points around me showed my relationship with all mankind: that I was influenced by their states and they were influenced by mine. If, therefore, I wanted to find my way to a state of peace and harmony in this world - and although my first responsibility must be my own state — I knew I would have to work for a state of peace and harmony in others.

"This understanding was followed by the wordless but clear knowledge that I had come into this life for one purpose only: to participate during my lifetime in a process and climactic event that would totally change the nature of man's life in this world — his culture, his governments, his laws, his economic activities.

"I knew that this would be brought about by a new and very powerful influx of the power of God similar to that at the time of Christ but modified to accord with the present state and needs of humanity. Later, I realised that this corresponded to what is called the Second Coming."

Mark went on to become a principal in various business enterprises in the United States, as well as in Australia and Latin America. He was also active as a nutritional scientist and as an adviser to various government bodies in the early 1940s.

In 1952 Mark underwent a second major spiritual experience, soon after which he began to receive interior locutions. These inner messages were in turn followed by 'memories' of experiences with Jesus two thousand years before, and by a sense of an increasing inner pressure to withdraw from his business activities and travel to Europe to 'look for somebody.'

Although at that time Mark was president of Collett-Week Corporation, a bulk producer of natural vitamins, and executive vice-president of Bacon Vulcanizer Manufacturing Company, a principal producer of equipment for re-treading and recapping tires, he resigned these posts and left for Europe. He carried with him letters of introduction to several notable personalities of the day, including well-known free market economists and certain intelligence operatives.

During his travels through Europe he continued to have experiences connected with the Second Coming, and in Paris one of his connections suggested he should visit a Monsieur Bernard Fay in Fribourg, Switzerland.

M. Fay, a Catholic and a former director of the French National Library, was at that time retired and living the life of a lay contemplative at Villa St. Jean in Fribourg. Mark, who was himself from a Protestant background, initiated their conversation by telling his host of his 1934 and 1952 experiences, as well as more recent interior locutions he had received in Latin, connected directly with the Roman Catholic Church.

Responding to his visitor's frank disclosures, M. Fay expressed the view that the depth of Mark's experiences revealed that he was clearly subject to the action of sanctifying grace, a condition that he, Fay, and certain friends in the faith were keenly seeking and praying for. The Frenchman then confided to Mark that he was very close to Pius XII and that he had in fact just returned from a stay of several months with him at Castel Gandolfo, the Pope's summer residence. Bernard Fay spoke of the Pontiff's fine spiritual qualities and then made an astounding reference to Fatima.

According to Fay, Pope Pius XII had brought Sister Lucia to Rome in 1950 and, under obedience, instructed her to reveal to him the Secret of Fatima, which she did. He went on:

"We know that we are about to see the Second Coming of Christ. We know that it will come from outside the Church and we know that it will come from the East."

He went on to tell Mark that all four of the then acknowledged mystics within the Church, recognized to be participating in the action of sanctifying grace – Sister Lucia herself, Padre Pio of Italy, Teresa Neumann of Germany and a French woman who could not be named – were receiving indications that pointed to the same conclusion.

◆ ◆ ◆

Mark received the latihan in New York in 1958, one of the first Americans to do so, and went on to play a key role both as a helper and as an administrator during the early days of Subud in the United States, including three terms as Chairman of Subud North America.

He met Bapak for the first time in 1959 and told him the full story of his experiences. Bapak's response to Mark's account of his meeting with Bernard Fay was "Yes." It was to be another nine years before Bapak was to throw fresh light on the subject, and, in a very real sense, the thrust of what he had to say was unintentionally corroborated by Pope John Paul II himself some twenty years later.

These talks that Bapak is giving
should not in any way be regarded
as a teaching; they are intended
only as explanations concerning
the way of spiritual progress.
You need them only in order that
your thoughts and feelings may
be able to become quiet.

Bapak
London, August 1959
(59 LON 5)

29

The Secret of Fatima, Part III

On 26 June 2000, the Congregation for the Doctrine of the Faith at the Vatican issued the following statement:

> Given below is the complete translation of the original Portuguese text of the third part of the secret of Fatima, revealed to the three shepherd children at Cova de Iria-Fatima on July 13 1917, and committed to paper by Sr. Lucia on January 3 1944.

> "I write in obedience to you, my God, who commands me to do so through His Excellency the Bishop of Leiria and through your Most Holy Mother and mine.

> "After the two parts which I have already explained, at the left of Our Lady and a little above, we saw an Angel with a flaming sword in his left hand; flashing, it gave out flames that looked as though they would set the world on fire, but they died out in contact with the splendour that Our Lady radiated towards him from her right hand. Pointing to the earth with his right hand, the Angel cried out in a loud voice: 'Penance, Penance, Penance!' And we saw an immense light that is God: 'something similar to how people appear in a mirror when they pass in front of it' a Bishop dressed in

white 'we had the impression that it was the Holy Father.' Other bishops, priests, men and women religious going up a steep mountain, at the top of which there was a big Cross of rough-hewn trunks as of a cork-tree with the bark. Before reaching there the Holy Father passed through a big city half in ruins and half trembling with halting step, afflicted with pain and sorrow, he prayed for the souls of the corpses he met on his way. Having reached the top of the mountain, on his knees at the foot of the big Cross, he was killed by a group of soldiers who fired bullets and arrows at him, and in the same way there died one after another of the other bishops, priests, men and women religious and various lay people of different ranks and positions. Beneath the two arms of the Cross there were two Angels, each with a crystal aspersorium in his hand, in which they gathered up the blood of the martyrs and with it sprinkled the souls that were making their way to God."

In conjunction with this publication of the purported Secret, the then-Cardinal Joseph Ratzinger (now Pope Benedict XVI) published a theological commentary, in which he asserted:

"A careful reading of the text of the so-called third 'secret' of Fatima ... will probably prove disappointing or surprising after all the speculation it has stirred. No great mystery is revealed; nor is the future unveiled."

This comment inevitably begs the question: given that "no great mystery is revealed; nor is the future unveiled" why oh why did the Church allow that very speculation to build up over so many decades? Why did so many Popes over such a long period of time clearly feel that it would be somehow prejudicial to the best interests of the Church to reveal the Secret? The published text hardly seems to merit such a sustained cover-up. Why was it okay to make public the other parts of the message of Fatima – relating to such enormous horrors as the Second World War, the rise of Communism and the annihilation of entire nations – but not okay to publish the admittedly blood-drenched call to penance now alleged to be the full extent of the Secret of Fatima?

Sadly, the Church's record does not predispose us to be able to accept all its public pronouncements on controversial issues at face value. In 1984, for example, after almost three years of research, David Yallop published his book *In God's Name,* in which he investigated the mysterious death of the 'Smiling Pope,' John Paul I, after just thirty-three days on the throne of Peter. Yallop concluded that the precise circumstances attending the discovery of the body "eloquently demonstrate that the Vatican practiced a disinformation campaign," that they told one lie after another: "Lies about little things, lies about big things . . . with but one purpose: to disguise the fact that Albino Luciani, Pope John Paul 1, had been assassinated."

For decades, the very same pattern of obfuscation has been playing out with regard to the Secret of Fatima, and there are many Catholics who still doubt that the full text has been revealed, prominent among them being The Fatima Centre, run by Father Nicholas Gruner, now officially suspended as a priest. It is beyond the scope of this book to go deeply into the debate. Instead, I would refer you to recently published books by two highly respected authors: lawyer and Catholic commentator Christopher A. Ferrara and leading journalist and TV anchor man Antonio Socci respectively. In their books *The Secret Still Hidden* and *Il Quarto Segreto di Fatima (The Fourth Secret of Fatima),* they both present a meticulous examination of the mass of available evidence, illustrating the tangled web of inconsistencies, excuses, prevarications and inadvertent admissions that characterizes this whole question. In the process, they totally demolish the specious arguments advanced by Vatican apologist Cardinal Tarcisio Bertone, who is forced to admit that there is actually a *second* envelope containing a text which has never been produced. This is believed to contain the actual words of Mary spoken to the three children at Fatima.

As already indicated, quite apart from the overwhelming body of closely reasoned argument advanced by Messrs Ferrara and Socci, I personally have three principal reasons for having come to this conclusion. Two of them will be well known to these authors; the third, and by far the most important, will not.

In the first place, there is simply no correlation between the content of the published text and Lucia's own statement that by 1960 the meaning of the message would appear "more clear." No events at that time can be said to correspond remotely with those that were foreshadowed in the official version.

The Pontiff himself concluded that the vision referred to an attempt on his own life, but again it is difficult to reconcile this view with the timing anticipated by Sister Lucia. The two attempts to kill the Pope – by the Turkish gunman Mehmet Ali Agca and the knife-wielding ultraconservative Spanish priest Juan Maria Fernandez y Krohn – took place in 1981 and 1982 respectively, long after the 1960 deadline for the release of the Secret.

To add to the confusion, in September 1983 the Montford Fathers of Bayshore New York, published an account of Pope John Paul II's interview with a small group of German Catholics. In response to a question about the Secret, the Holy Father said, "Because of the seriousness of its contents . . . my Predecessors in the Chair of Peter have diplomatically preferred to withhold its publication. On the other hand, it should be sufficient for all Christians to know this much: if there is a message in which it is said that the oceans will flood entire sections of the earth; that, from one moment to the other, millions of people will perish...there is no longer any point in really wanting to publish this secret message." Again, this scenario bears no relation to the official version that was eventually made public.

The second reason I believe it is reasonable to suspect that the whole truth has still not emerged is implicit in yet another statement by John Paul II, this time in response to questions from the Italian media in the mid-1980s. On this occasion, although there is absolutely nothing in the published version to open the door for anyone to put themselves forward, His Holiness said that he did not wish to reveal the Secret because it would "encourage false prophets." With this remark, although he would have had no way of knowing it, he could be said to be endorsing what Bapak had told the Weeks some twenty years before.

Which brings us to the third reason I believe we have not been told the whole truth about the Secret of Fatima: a reason which one can well imagine could have shocked and terrified the Church authorities, precipitating the initial 1960 statement that it "would not be published, and probably never would be."

◆ ◆ ◆

Twice during 1963 Bapak stayed with the Weeks in Briarcliff, New York, and during these periods Mark's association with Bapak became very close. Later, Bapak asked Mark to move to Indonesia to be near him, and in 1965 Mark and Istimah, together with their two children, David and Sandra, went to live next to him in Jakarta. Some months after their arrival, because of attacks on the Subud compound by Communist guerillas at a time of severe political insecurity, Bapak suggested to Mark that he temporarily move his family to New Zealand.

During a tour in 1968, Bapak stayed for ten days with Mark and Istimah in their New Zealand home. He was accompanied by his wife, Ibu, his interpreter, Usman, and Usman's wife, Aminah. On the last day of his visit, said Istimah, and seemingly quite out of the blue, Bapak – full name Muhammad Subuh Sumohadiwidjojo - brought up the subject of Fatima.

"Whenever Bapak stayed with us," Istimah told me, "he would invariably present us with a special gift, usually in the form of new insight of a spiritual nature.

"I was doing something in the kitchen on the morning of Bapak's departure. Aminah was with me, and maybe one other Subud member. Usman was in the adjoining dining area having breakfast.

"Suddenly, to our surprise, in the middle of these domestic activities, Bapak entered the kitchen, looking very relaxed in his shirt sleeves. He sat in the lounge area near to where Usman was drinking his coffee, his back to the window with its beautiful view of the Gulf of Hauraki. He started to talk to us about the secret of Fatima, and I knew at once that this was his inner present to us on this occasion.

"We all stopped what we were doing, while Usman translated intermittently in order to avoid interrupting Bapak.

"Bapak talked for some time about the miracle at Fatima and said that the message contained the information that salvation would come with a man from the East, and that his name was Muhammad."

30

The Vatican

In 1992 and again in 1997, much exercised by all the information that had come their way, Istimah and Mark Week, in collaboration with close family friend Raymond van Sommers, repeatedly sought to bring it to the attention of the Vatican.

In the next few pages, by kind permission of Raymond and of Mark and Istimah's daughter Sandra, I am able to reproduce copies of this correspondence. This includes a letter from Istimah to Pope John Paul II, a letter from Mark to Raymond van Sommers in which he makes reference to Bernard Fay and a letter from Raymond to the then Cardinal Ratzinger.

Both Istimah's book *The Man From The East* – co-authored with Raymond van Sommers - and Raymond's own *A Life in Subud* are enthralling Subud memoirs. Both are obtainable from Subud Publications International.

Letter from Istimah Week to Pope John Paul II

Mrs. Istimah Week
857 Samara Way
Carlsbad, CA 92009
U.S.A.

To His Holiness
Pope John Paul II
Vatican City
Rome, Italy

January 7, 1992

Your Holiness,

With the utmost respect, I write this letter to Your Holiness to request a personal audience.

I do so without willful intention, but in obedience to the promptings of my inner feeling to convey to Your Holiness information of extreme importance for mankind.

With humility before the Greatness of Almighty God, I submit that there is in the world a new possibility of a contact with Sanctifying Grace, which through Your Holiness could flood into the souls of millions of people.

I speak of a contact with the Power of God which I have experienced, and followed its effects and guidance for some 33 years.

It has the characteristics of the action of the Holy Spirit as received in the Church by the Saints but which is now miraculously available to ordinary souls who ask for it. It is transmitted from person to person by inner contact in a state of sincere submission and trust in Almighty God.

The Divine Grace received purifies the whole being and brings a person into a state of worship of Almighty God beyond the effort of the heart and mind, but by His Will and by His Grace.

This possibility, which spread to a small number of people throughout the world from 1957, and is now practiced by some 10,000 people, awaits unused by humanity as a whole.

I feel that Your Holiness should know of this, so that, if it is God's Will, it could come to the world through the Church and Your Holy Person.

It is because I cannot adequately explain this receiving in a letter, that I beg Your Holiness to grant me an audience.

With my love and devotion,

Istimah Week

Istimah Week

Note: Istimah did not receive a reply to this letter

Letter from Mark Week to Raymond van Sommers

27 January 97

Dear Raymond,

I read the English translation of the news interview with Ratzinger whilst he was in Portugal. I had understood it quite well in the original report. I am not really so interested, except to see how the Vatican is rationalizing their refusal to release the report (Third Secret) in the form written by Sister Lucia herself. In a way, their reasoning is right, because there would immediately appear a plethora of claims to identity of the 'Second Coming' coming from the East. Also, Ratzinger is saying that the important thing for the individual is prayer and faith — and for most, this is probably true. It is all they can do, and it will help (some). Further, he says that the "Madonna is not a sensationalist, doesn't provoke fears, and doesn't make apocalyptic predictions". Well, why does he say that? Surely because that can be an interpretation of parts of her 'Third Secret'. Many people equate the 'Second Coming' with the 'end of the world'. And Sister Lucia answered questions about the 'Third Secret', saying "Some people will be very happy; some will be very sad". The 'sad' people will certainly feel 'threatened'. It is all in the point of view.

to p2

Page 2 - 27 Jan 97 - Mark to Raymond

I am not very interested in writing to Cardinal Ratzinger, but it may very well be appropriate for you to do so, with a copy of the Book.

The point is, the Book will not tell Ratzinger ~~anything~~ about the Secret itself. The present Pope knows everything that Pope John XXIII knew, and everything that Pope Pius XII knew. They know who Bernard Fay is, also. That is, 'they' brackets Ratzinger with Pope John Paul II. It is likely, however, that he might find points of other interest in the 'Book' (if he reads it).

Ratzinger and the present Pope _do_ convey their fealty to the Madonna — and 'they' are taking 'Her' very seriously — meaning also that they are taking the 'Third Secret' very seriously.

Love, Mark

Transcription of letter from Mark Week to Raymond van Sommers

27 January 1997

Dear Raymond,

I read the English translation of the news interview with [Cardinal] Ratzinger whilst he was in Portugal. I had understood it quite well in the original report. I am not really so interested, except to see how the Vatican is rationalizing their refusal to release the report (Third Secret) in the form written by Sister Lucia herself.

In a way, their reasoning is right, because there would immediately appear a plethora of claims to identity of the 'Second Coming' coming from the East. Also, Ratzinger is saying that the important thing for the individual is prayer and faith— and for most, this is probably true. It is all they can do, and it will help (some). Further he says that the "Madonna is not sensationalist, doesn't provoke fears, and doesn't make apocalyptic predictions." Well, why does he say that? Surely because that can be an interpretation of parts of her 'Third Secret'. Many people equate the 'Second Coming' with 'the end of the world'. And sister Lucia answered questions about the 'Third Secret' saying "Some people will be very happy; some will be very sad". The 'sad' people will certainly feel 'threatened'. It's all in the point of view.

I am not very interested in writing to Ratzinger, but it may very well be appropriate for you to do so, with a copy of the Book [The Man From The East].

The point is, the Book will not tell Ratzinger anything about the Secret itself. The present Pope knows everything that Pope John XXII knew, and everything that Pope Pius XII knew. They know who Bernard Fay is, also. That is, 'they' brackets Cardinal Ratzinger with Pope John Paul II. It is likely, however, that he might find points of other interest in the Book (if he reads it).

[Cardinal] Ratzinger and the present Pope do convey their fealty to the Madonna— and 'they' are taking 'Her' very seriously—meaning also that they are taking the 'Third Secret' very seriously.

Love
Mark

2 February 1997

His Eminence Joseph Cardinal Ratzinger
Prefect of the Congregation for the Doctrine of the Faith
Curia Vescovile
Piazza Caduti Sul Lavoro, 6
00049 Velletri Italy

Your Eminence

It was with great interest that I followed the interview of Your Eminence by Radio Renascença in Fatima, on the occasion of the 79th Anniversary of the last apparition of Our Lady.

When I heard that Your Eminence was privileged to have knowledge of the content of the third message of Our Lady of Fatima to Sister Lucia I felt that I should send you a copy of the enclosed book THE MAN FROM THE EAST by Istimah Week.

The book mentions the third message of Our Lady of Fatima (pages 7 and 73) when in 1953 the author's husband met with M. Bernard Fay, at that time a Catholic contemplative residing in Fribourg, Switzerland. Mr. Week was experiencing visions and revelations having to do with the Second Coming. At the time of their meeting, M. Fay had just returned from the Castel Gandolfo, where he had spent several months as a guest of His Holiness Pope Pius XII.It was only after Mr. Week had spoken of the content of his own experiences that M. Fay felt confident to reveal as much as he did. As well as speaking of the 'third message', M. Fay revealed that he himself had experienced seeing through His Holiness Pope Pius XII while in the gardens of the Castel (as through a pane of glass), and also that Pope Pius XII had experienced apparitions of Christ on two occasions.

I submit the book in the belief that it might contain some other points of interest to Your Eminence.

Most respectfully yours

Raymond van Sommers.

Raymond van Sommers
Co-author

Note: Cardinal Ratzinger replied with a thank-you card for the gift

31

The Second Coming

The very last thing I intend with this book is that it should degenerate into a litany of charges of a lack of transparency against one of the great bulwarks of a world-renowed religion. Although I am not a Catholic, my latihan has resonated deeply with the unmistakable spiritual essence pervading Catholic churches and shrines all over the world.

Indeed, once the initial decision had been taken by the Vatican not to reveal the full truth about the Secret of Fatima, one can only have compassion for the dilemma in which successive Church hierarchies would have found themselves. Given what Bernard Fay confided to Mark Week, it is not difficult to sympathise with the defensive anxiety that would have been aroused by intimations that the Second Coming would come from 'outside the Church.'

That said, and taking into account what Bapak told the Weeks in New Zealand in 1968 and what John Bennett received at the monastery of St. Wandrille in 1959 – "It is My Will that My Church and Islam should be united" – what a truly mind-blowing prospect for religious unification may well have been held out to the world in the shape of the Secret of Fatima, namely:

that the long-awaited Second Coming of Christ, foretold both by Biblical scribes and by the Prophet of Islam, is now with us; that it is embodied in a contact sent to mankind through a Muslim, a man from the East, and intended to be announced to the world by the Queen of Christendom, the one person revered by both religions, the one person capable of uniting Christianity and Islam.

At no time, incidentally, did Bapak ever seek to allege that he himself was the personification of the Second Coming; indeed, in all his thousands of talks around the world he scarcely made reference to the subject. On the contrary, whereas in the past, he said, the grace and guidance of the power of God was usually made available to mankind through a prophet or messenger, with the latihan it is as if "God Himself has got up off His throne and come down to earth."

In one rather more specific reference, he said:

In Christianity it has been said that Christ has already come down to earth. This is not the Christ that you see in pictures, for he has come down to human beings themselves at this time. Indeed, in Christianity it has become known that something will arise in the East that signals the return of Jesus Christ to earth and from here it will spread.

As to spreading word of this amazing Grace, in 1981, in a letter to American Subud member, Maria Baker, agreeing to her proposal that a documentary film should be made about Subud – a project that, for practical reasons, never came to fruition – Bapak wrote:

Bapak had wanted to wait until the fruits of the latihan were really evident before publicising Subud, but because of the world situation it is too late and

we must begin to let people know about Subud now. If we wait until the evidence is really convincing, it will take too long. This is a change, because until now Subud has been hidden.

In the same year, he gave a talk in which he said,

Bapak does not like to use the word *sin*, but at least it is a very great mistake if this spiritual exercise does not spread to the whole of mankind; if it gets stuck with just a few people here and there.

I recall Mark Week telling me about a gathering of men helpers in Jakarta at which Bapak went around the circle indicating to each person what their individual role should be in the spreading of Subud and its establishment in the world. To Mark, for example, Bapak said that he should be instrumental in the setting up of major international centres. Bapak told another brother, a very gifted writer and communicator and a high profile figure in the Subud organization, that he should be writing books about Subud that would reach the general public. None of the people involved, Mark freely admitted, went on to fulfill the role that Bapak held out to them. Most of them are now dead, a notable exception being Raymond van Sommers, already mentioned in these pages, who is very much alive and well and living in Australia. A close friend of the Weeks and co-author of Istimah's book *The Man From The East,* Raymond was a key witness to some of the events I chronicle herein.

As a result of my crisis experiences and other indications, I too felt a definite sense of mission on behalf of Bapak, a responsibility attested to by Sudarto. As with Mark and the others, however, and despite my best efforts back in 1991, this has not yet been realised. But it has never died. On the contrary, it has deepened and broadened over the years, and I am now fully committed to this third attempt to get this message out to the world.

The import of the correlation between my own receiving at Medjugorje and the reported indications being received by all four Catholic mystics at the time of Mark Week's meeting with Bernard Fay is just too important not to be accorded the widest possible dissemination.

That said, however, and despite all the facts I have brought together in the last few chapters of this book, my conviction in seeking to 'spread the word' is not dependent upon any external source nor upon anything that has been said by any other human being. It is founded upon the experiences that have been given to me, many of which – to use the designation that Bapak once characterized as the hallmark of true spiritual experiences - were "one hundred times more real than our everyday reality."

Typical of this was the receiving at Medjugorje that the latihan is a manifestation of the Second Coming. This indication came as a complete surprise. It was not at all what I was looking for, hoping for or expecting. It did not arise in my heart or in my mind or even within my inner self. It came down from above and entered my being like a column of knowledge.

Experiences such as this are more real than any book, more to be believed than any belief system, more to be trusted than anything that can be said by any mortal being. Because of this, I *know* beyond any doubt that the latihan is a manifestation of the Second Coming. Given the precise wording of the revelation, however – namely, that it is *a* manifestation – I certainly cannot aver that it is the entirety of that event. It may well be that it is but one particularly potent and direct expression of a global shift in consciousness that is destined to lift mankind to a state of Being truly worthy of being called human.

32

The Christ

Although for years I had uttered the name *Christus* in latihan, not since I was a child had I experienced any real sense of the validity of the person of Jesus, or indeed of the religion that is named after Him. In late 1989, however, I became aware of the emergence within me of a great mystery. It began when I awoke to find myself saying aloud, "The *coming* of the Christ," and continued throughout 1990 with an increasing awareness of the *reality* of the Christ.

After my experiences at Medjugorje my latihan had deepened, and at the end of one particularly profound latihan I received "The Christ is in you to His full power," to which, from another place within me, I responded, "I know that *I* have to go, for *Him.*" This was followed by a renewal of my inner pledge to follow wherever God might lead – a sure sign of 'interesting' times ahead!

And so it proved to be. Immediately after this experience I had to spend hours, day and night, in latihan, moving through seemingly impenetrable blockages, sustained by the constant inner prayer that arose of itself within me. One night in particular it was as if the devil himself had to vacate yet another unsuspected area within me, which he was most reluctant to do!

The next night I awoke to feel both my hands held in a firm but unseen grip and I received a latihan of great sweetness and consolation and knew that I was beloved of God.

While emerging from the crisis I had had a particularly clear dream in which I was cruising from deep in space towards earth, but it was not the ordinary me. I was aglow with glory, with extraordinary light and power blazing from and through me. I was moving at a very steady pace as if in tune with a pre-ordained plan or timetable. I wore what seemed to be a stiff cape that protruded outward on each side like partly folded wings. When I mentioned this experience to Sudarto in Jakarta, he had replied rather sharply "First you have to pass through all the other levels," as if to caution me against the risk of getting inflated ideas about my spiritual progress.

In September 1990, I had a dream in which my skin was beginning to burst at the seams, revealing nothing but light and power within. In a solitary latihan not long afterwards I experienced what I can only describe as a complete identification with the Christ within me.

This single episode, which felt totally natural and lasted for about half an hour, seemed at the time like the consummation and purpose of all my experiences until that point. It imbued me with fresh inspiration and a new perspective with which to return to the manuscript I had set aside after the apparition of Mary in May. In all my prior experiences, both before, during and immediately after I visited Medjugorje, I had experienced the presence of Christ in the form of visions separate from and external to my own being. Now I was beginning to experience an inner oneness with this presence.

I awoke early one morning in December 1990 to see my body composed entirely of blazing light. Attached to it were two enormous wings.

I did not mention this last fact in the original version of my book. For one thing, I knew it would sound far-fetched, even crazy, and for another I did not want people to think I was on an ego trip, which is indeed a constant trap when one is obliged to use the mind to tell of such things. Now, however, in 2009, in the interests of bearing true witness and perhaps of validating similar experiences that others may have received, I am sharing it. Looking back, I can see that, to borrow from Sufi terminology, experiences like this, together with others that were to follow, would have been manifestations of temporary states rather than of a permanent station.

During one latihan in 2003, for example, on the evening of the fifteenth day of Ramadan, the exact mid-point of the fast, I was blessed to be taken over by an Identity far beyond anything I could have imagined, one that at the time I could only sustain for about ten minutes. It was but a taste, but it was accompanied by the clearest possible indication that this level of Being would one day reign supreme within me.

Meanwhile, by the end of 1990 I had more or less ended my book – or so I thought – with the conclusion of my visit to Medjugorje. Although my inner experiences continued to develop in delicate and intimate harmony with the being of Christ, I felt that I neither cared nor dared to talk about them. But when I showed my manuscript to a few Subud friends, I was encouraged to find that it seemed to give them confidence to share with me their own similar, if not identical, experiences. One in particular, a Jewish film maker, told me that she had experienced the reality of oneness with Christ within herself more than fifteen years before, shortly after she had been opened. She too had rarely found it possible to speak of this experience to anyone else.

Like her, I had found it impossible to speak of these deeply personal, precious and rather incredible things to more than a few very close friends. That I am now sharing as much as feels right with whoever may be moved to read my story is because I came to realize that it was not enough for me to have received that the latihan is a manifestation of the Second Coming. I knew that I had to have the courage to bear witness to it by including in this account my own experiences of the reality of the Christ within my being.

No words of mine can penetrate this ineffable mystery. In seeking to express the inexpressible, I can do no better than fall back upon the simple eloquence of St. Paul. His *I live, yet not I, but Christ liveth in me* is, in my experience, given new life two thousand years later in this wondrous latihan: in this spiritual exercise in which I move and smile, love and worship. In which I move . . . yes, and yet not I.

My experiences continued to affirm the validity of Paul's vision. In one, a voice in the night said to me, "Christ is the strength in you." In another, a twofold experience, I was first made aware of the Christ in me reaching out, often in quite small ways, to touch and help others, and then of the Christ in others reaching out to touch and help me.

I am coming to believe that when Jesus said, "I and the Father are one," He was pointing to the ever deeper spiritual realization that awaits all of us. I am sometimes given to glimpse these depths for myself in latihan, in which *I* am *Him*, and in which I know that I am an extension of God's will and purpose.

It is important to add that this self-same spiritual reality – so much deeper than the mere labels and concepts with which we reflect and express them – could easily be described differently by people of diverse backgrounds, by Muslims, Hindus, Sikhs, Jews, Buddhists, etc., etc.

I would not have the temerity to give voice to these mysteries were it not for the direct simplicity of Bapak himself. It is not that Almighty God *Himself* is within us, he explained in Vancouver in July 1981, but that the *power* of God is within everything He created within the whole universe. He continued:

> The only difference is which of His creatures are aware of the presence of the power of God and which of them are not aware of it. This is the distinction that becomes apparent in the latihan . . . you are able to become aware of the presence, the manifestation, of God's power within you. Within our being this power enables us to get to know and to feel our own true nature and personality, like a life within your life and deeper than your everyday life.
> **It is this which you must magnify. It is this which must be your God. Because there is nothing else from which you can learn. There is nothing else that you can follow except this reality that is within you.**

Writing this book is very much an exercise in doing just that, despite the fact that it may well be controversial: among some Muslims, among some Christians and, not least, within Subud itself. Controversy is one thing; causing offence is quite another – and I ask forgiveness of anyone who may be offended by any aspect of my story.

◆ ◆ ◆

In March 1990 I spent ten days in Jakarta attending the final ceremony commemorating Bapak's death, held exactly one thousand days after his passing. During that visit, while maintaining a one and a half hour vigil at Bapak's graveside, I was suddenly taken far out into space where I was met by Our Lady. I greeted her, oh so gently – "Mary." – not as a distant iconic figure, but rather as the sweetest of sisters. Looking back at the tiny planet earth far below, I saw that my view of it was almost entirely eclipsed by this book

The next day, some three years after I heard Bapak say into my ear that one day he would tell me my real name, I received deeply within myself that my name should be changed to Emmanuel. As a matter of courtesy – since she had given me the name Marius – I confirmed the truth of this receiving with Ibu Rahayu, Bapak's daughter.

One month later I learned the meaning of the other name Bapak had called me in a dream of some ten years before. He had called me *Parousia* and it was only now, quite by chance, that I discovered that this was a Greek word meaning Second Coming. Clearly, Bapak must have foreseen that, in writing this book, I would be guided to share with you the revelation that the latihan is indeed a manifestation of the Second Coming of Christ, a reality in which all men and women everywhere may participate here and now.

Commenting on the nature of all that had happened to me, Bapak's daughter Ibu Rahayu wrote:

> "You became a tool of the power of the One Almighty God, meaning you were able to make use of your power of observation, which was filled by the power of God, so that you could be a witness to how great is the power of God and how small we as human beings are."

This is what I have tried to do in these pages: to bear witness to a great truth, with all the sincerity I can muster and always on my guard against the subtle ways in which the ego of this 'small human being' would like to have its way, an intent in which I have inevitably failed to some extent. Bringing this book to a close feels very akin to signing off a personal letter to you, Dear Reader, so please allow me to conclude by sending you Love and wishing you every blessing on your journey Home.

Your brother,
Emmanuel

Postscript

Every personal letter worthy of the name should have a P.S. at the end, and I feel it is particularly warranted in this case.

You have just read what one early reader of this manuscript described as a "high octane spiritual adventure story," and I feel it's important to balance it as best as I can. It is, after all, just one man's experience in reaction to being touched by what Bapak once called the most powerful force in the universe. It is essential, once again, to stress that everyone's experience in receiving this Grace will be different and will be entirely in keeping with their own nature; may well indeed, as in most cases, be a very gentle progression when compared with what happened to me.

My 'intersection' with Mary in particular, for example, was a highly individual dimension of my own personal journey. Powerful and highly significant though it was for Emmanuel Elliott, it may well mean nothing to most other Subud members, or indeed to you too should you ever choose to ask for the contact. Whatever might unfold within *you* in response to being 'opened' would be an expression of your own unique inner being, entirely free of the beliefs and opinions of anyone else.

To help you appreciate the sheer universality of Subud, to give you an insight into the experiences and attitudes of a diversity of Subud members, I urge you to visit Simón Cherpitel's superb photographic panorama at www.subud-world.com, where he has brilliantly captured the Subud ambience in a series of short quotes from Subud members the world over against a backdrop of stunning pictures.

For Simón's equally evocative homage to Bapak himself, spanning his world travels from 1969 to 1981, go to www.subuh.com. Both sites are atmospheric labours of love, created by a dedicated Subud brother who also happens to be an outstanding professional photographer.

To find out about Subud in your country, go to www.subud.com and click on Subud and then on Subud Contacts. Scroll down and you will find your country listed in one of nine zones. Click on it and you will be able to access an email address for your national chairperson. He or she will be able to direct you to your nearest local group, where you will receive a warm welcome, as well as answers to any questions that this book may have raised. Should you decide that Subud may be for you, all you have to do is ask to receive the contact.

Blessings,
E.E.

Appendix A

The Benedictine Connection

As already reported in Chapter 24, in 1959 three of the monks at the St. Wandrille monastery received the contact from John Bennett. In 1962, one of them, the Reverend Albert-Jacques Bescond, contributed two articles to a Subud periodical of the time, extracts from which are combined hereunder. Father Bescond died in 1986.

He wrote:

"For more than a year I have been asked to testify. The questions put to me can be reduced to two. I shall try to answer them by expressing something of what, over a period of three years, I have received from the latihan.

"I hope that these words may bring a little light and peace of mind to those Catholics who have need of them. Certainly I would not wish to impose my own experience as a line of conduct to be followed by others, and still less would I wish to dogmatise and state 'the attitude of the Church.'

"In fact, I am not authorized to do that, nor is there anything spectacular about my Subud experience. Undoubtedly as soon as I received the contact I was cured of vertigo, and I found myself able to swim. But after all a monk might hope for more than that.

"I must add that the practice of the latihan has built up in me a very solid stability, a deep rooting in my vocation as a monk. In particular the reality of the Mystical Body and of the transfer of merits, which can alone justify withdrawal into the monastic life, have become for me a matter of direct experience. They are like a climate in which one lives, like the air one breathes.

"All religions are in a state of expectation: each, in its manner, is awaiting a state of Advent, a mysterious Easter which will perhaps not dawn until the Last Day."

♦ ♦ ♦

Although Bapak himself did not visit the Monastery, he did reply to some written questions put to him by the monks:

Q. Is the Force of Life to be regarded as a person? Can one speak of it in the depths of one's heart, or is it an impersonal principle?
A. The Great Life Force is not personal. It penetrates everything that exists, from the purest essence to the coarsest matter. It is not a separate being, such as for example the Pure Soul, that of the 7th degree, which can neither touch nor be touched by matter. The Great Life Force enters everywhere.

Q. If he who practices the latihan permits himself to indulge in bad conduct, does this interfere with the action of the latihan in him, and is he more culpable than someone who does not practice the latihan and succumbs to the same temptations?
A. A judge who commits an illegal act is more guilty than someone who does not know the law. In the latihan you receive a light which enables you to recognize the true nature of

your own acts. If you act against the light, you are more culpable than someone who does not have the light.

Q. If in the course of the latihan I have an experience which enables me to understand certain things, and which leads me to take corresponding decisions, should I follow this experience if it is in opposition to the authority of the Church?
A. In the first place, it should be said that one should not accept indications which come to us in the latihan, so long as our own thought, our own feeling and our own desires are involved.
Long practice and considerable purification of the soul are needed before the soul is fit to receive valid illuminations. It is therefore better to put this aside and not concern oneself with indications that come to us whether in the course of the latihan or otherwise.

Furthermore, as for any contradiction that might arise between what is received as a private illumination and those which have been received in the past and which have formed the doctrine of the Church, in principle, since they come from the same Source, there should never be any contradiction. But we are men, and we can err. Therefore patience and obedience are necessary. But if there comes an illumination which is truly from the Holy Spirit, it will come in such a manner that it will be impossible to reject it. At the root of the matter, our obedience is towards the Will of God alone.

Appendix B

What is Subud?

**Once the whole of your inner feeling has been
brought to life, you will be able to feel your true nature.
Then you will be able to tell what is right for you and
what is not, which part of you is noble and which is
base, and which part of you is your true individuality.
You will know the true way to behave. This is what this
latihan is for - it has come from God; it is God's help.**

Bapak, New York City, 18 May 1967

The term Subud is a contraction of three Sanskrit words –
Susila, Budhi and *Dharma* – which can be summarized to mean
'right living from within according to the will of God.' Another
explanation is that when the name was first received, it brought
with it its own meaning: namely, 'from God, through God, back
to God.'

At the heart of Subud is the *latihan kejiwaan*, two Indonesian
words that simply mean 'spiritual exercise.' Exercise (or 'training') is the English word that comes closest to expressing the
meaning of the Indonesian word *latihan*, although most Subud
people still prefer to use the original word latihan.

The way of the latihan is a way of purification and self-realisation, based upon a way of self-realisation, based upon total surrender to Almighty God. It is a way that progresses of itself from a source deep within a person's inner being as a result of nothing less than a direct personal contact with the power of God.

One's particular concept of God, or how one may define God, is not itself pertinent to the latihan experience itself. In fact, those uncomfortable with concepts like God and the will of God might well express this same reality in terms of their own choosing and understanding. They might instead speak of devotion to Truth; of harmonizing with the vital essence at the heart of all creation; of uniting with that love and light in which all is one; of merging with the Life that is both unimaginably vast and universal and at the same time inexpressibly personal and near.

This latihan or spiritual exercise, was first received by Muhammad Subuh Sumohadiwodjojo, the man now known around the world simply as Bapak. He originally called it 'training for human life,' but later changed the name to 'spiritual training,' to which people seemed better able to relate.

For the purposes of this book, my treatment of Bapak's life will cover only the basic essentials. For the full story I would refer the reader to Bapak's autobiography, published posthumously at his request by Subud Publications International, England. Over the years, S.P.I. has also published a wide range of excellent books on Subud.[1]

Bapak was born at dawn on June 22 1901 and died at dawn on June 23, 1987. His birth was preceded and accompanied by many signs and portents, and from his earliest days it was clear that he was indeed a man of destiny.

---

[1] http://www.subudbooks.net

He was drawn to the quest for the perfect life from an early age, but was told by local gurus that he already carried within him that which he sought and that this would be revealed to him of itself when the time was right.

In 1925, aged 24, Bapak was out walking one night when a brilliant ball of light descended from the sky and entered his body, a light that lit up the whole countryside and was witnessed by many people in the locality. The light initiated a strong vibration within his being, a manifestation of the Great Life Force which, years later, he was to speak of in the following terms:

> This vibration, this power we experience after the opening, is the vibration that exists within all things, within the whole universe. It is the basis or the beginning of the whole universe. In the Christian religion, this power or this vibration that we receive in the latihan is called the Holy Ghost.

When this power arose within him, Bapak's first thought was that he must be suffering a heart attack. He returned home and lay down, expecting to die. Instead, he was moved to stand up and pray. Thus did Bapak receive the very first latihan, a special state that was to arise within him every night thereafter for the next three years. Throughout this time he hardly slept, while continuing to maintain a job and all other normal responsibilities of family and daily life.

During these years of continuous nightly latihan, Bapak encountered an infinite variety of inner and outer experiences, as an extraordinary process of spiritual transformation and realisation unfolded within him. Eight years later, after a spiritual ascension that took him 'through all the heavens,' Bapak was guided to understand that it was his mission to transmit this inner contact to all who asked for it.

So began the spread of Subud, starting with those of Bapak's inner circle of friends and fellow seekers who wished to join him in following the latihan, and going on to reach many parts of Indonesia during the next twenty years.

Though Bapak's inner guidance had indicated that the time would come when he would travel the world on behalf of Subud he was content to remain in Indonesia until 1957, when he accepted an invitation to visit London as the guest of a small group of Westerners, a few of whom had already been opened in Cyprus by Husein Rofe.

Shortly after his arrival in England, he was invited to take up residence at Coombe Springs, the Surrey home of John Bennett, where his visit happened to coincide with an international Gurdjieff seminar. It was there that the latihan met with an immediate and enthusiastic response that resulted in scores of overseas visitors returning home to spread the contact. Many of these in their turn invited Bapak to visit their own countries, and his planned short visit to England developed into a world tour that lasted for fourteen months. Amid this flurry of activity and excitement, the *latihan* found its way to Europe, the Americas and Australia.

Bapak's visit to the West in 1957 proved to be the first of many. For the rest of his life he maintained a tireless commitment to a succession of world journeys, giving lengthy explanations about the *latihan* to the steadily growing international membership that today exists in more than seventy countries.

Bapak consistently emphasized that Subud is not a religion. In fact, he urged Subud members who do adhere to a religion to remain true to their own faith. He described the latihan as the spiritual reality that lies at the heart of all the great religions: the inner truth for which seekers in every age have yearned. It has come at a time, he often said, when mankind in general finds it difficult to sustain a simple faith in God based purely upon the teaching and advice contained in the holy books, a time when many people consider a specific religion to be too restrictive.

He often reminded us that the latihan is a gift beyond value, a timely intervention from on high that has come about in our era precisely because the increasingly powerful influence of the material life force now seriously threatens the peace and very survival of the world.

◆ ◆ ◆

**You are guided in only one direction: towards God.
And the way is through the purity, goodness and
nobility of your inner self.**
- Bapak

The tapes and transcripts of Bapak's talks over the years possess a radiant content and clarity. They project an authority and wisdom that bear eloquent witness to the source of his guidance. In Los Angeles, in July 1981, for example, Bapak said:

The thing that most affects our life and the result of our life is our character. And it is precisely this that can be changed by the latihan exercise.

In this exercise we truly experience things that human beings in general cannot or do not experience, which lead to a change, an improvement, a correction or repair to our character. And this repair is something that can only be done by the power of Almighty God. For example, if you have a person who lacks a feeling of love for his fellow human beings, this lack – which is a flaw in his character – is truly what is called a sickness of the soul. This is the deep sickness we all worry about – the real sickness is the inability of a person to love other people and to feel compassion for other people.

Now it is this lack that can be cured by the latihan exercise and this is something that generally is not possible for a human being, to cure or heal her or his character. Brothers and Sisters, at this moment this illness of the character that

Bapak has described is playing havoc in the world without people in general being aware of it. The world in this situation cannot be brought to a state of peace unless this illness of the character can be cured. This is why this latihan is so important, so crucial for mankind today, because it enables us to change something within ourselves that cannot be changed in the normal course of events.

For some, such a transformation happens quickly; for others more slowly, depending upon one's own character flaws and those that we inherit from our ancestors. Patience is the key, said Bapak: we need to persevere and surrender, with patience and sincerity.

Inevitably, Bapak's talks also testify to the spiritual stature of the man himself, although he never held himself out to be anything other than an ordinary man. It was this humility and down-to-earth quality that so characterised Bapak. Always concerned with differentiating between the message and the messenger, he consistently emphasized the importance of following the latihan and surrendering only to God.

Although increasingly in later years Bapak encouraged people to write about their Subud experiences, he did not believe that the latihan should be promoted or publicized. "The latihan should spread by example, not by advertising," he said. The Subud association, therefore, grew slowly and steadily, almost solely by word of mouth and by the positive changes brought about in the characters and lives of those who had received and continued to follow the latihan.

When Bapak died in 1987, there were Subud groups scattered throughout the world, with a total active membership of approximately 10,000 otherwise ordinary people whose only apparent common denominator is the fact that they have received the contact. Many of them never got to see or hear Bapak for themselves. The affairs of the Subud association are looked after by a loosely knit affiliation of group, regional, national and international committees, set up, in Bapak's words, "to serve the latihan." Basic functions of this committee structure, therefore, include the provision of accommodation in which to do latihan, the organization of periodic congresses at the various levels – international, national and regional - and the dissemination of information about Subud and the latihan.

Through congresses and a variety of newsletters and other publications, the Subud association also provides a framework for networking on the myriad welfare, youth and cultural activities in which many of the members are involved. Since participation in the organisational side of Subud is entirely voluntary, being a member of Subud need involve no more than simply turning up for latihan.

◆ ◆ ◆

Today, there are Subud groups in or near most major cities around the world.[1] Generally speaking, these groups remain quite small, but all include people well established in the latihan. It can be said, therefore, that the foundation has been laid for a significant increase in the membership. It is the duty of some of these experienced men and women, known as helpers, to serve as witnesses in enabling newcomers to receive the same direct contact with the power of God, with the Great Life Force, that Bapak himself first received.

All that is required for this 'opening' and the consequent awakening of the inner self, to be effected is for the applicant to stand quietly with a feeling of patience and surrender in the presence of others doing the latihan. One of the helpers will read the following statement to the new person:

> We are helpers in the spiritual association of Subud, and we are here to be as witnesses to your wish to worship the One

---

[1] http://subudworldnews.com/hotlinks/index.php

Almighty God. We hope that your wish is truly based on sincerity.

You know that the One Almighty God is the Creator of the whole universe, of all that can be seen as well as all that cannot be seen with our ordinary eyes. God is All-Glorious, All-Knowing and All-Powerful. Therefore, in your worship, to which we bear witness, it will not be right to make use of your own self-willed desires and thoughts. For this reason, we hope that at this moment you do not concentrate your thoughts, but open your feelings, truly surrender and submit your own will to the will of God, and be patient and sincere before the glory and greatness of the One Almighty God.

Would you repeat after me: I believe in the One Almighty God and wish to worship only God.

So that your feelings can become calm, we would like you to close your eyes, to stand quite relaxed and to pay no attention to other people exercising. Also, when movement arises within your body, to not resist it and do not feel anxiety, but freely follow whatever arises within you.

After their opening, many people are immediately aware that something special and unexpected has happened to them. Others may have to wait some time before being able to feel the direct action of their own latihan.

Helpers also have the responsibility for passing on the clarifications and guidelines Bapak gave about following the latihan. They will explain that it works and progresses in a process that is unique to each individual and totally in harmony with his or her own nature and needs. It is unconfined by dogma and is free of hierarchical interpretation or authority. It is real: its effectiveness undiminished by space and time, its endurance unaffected by Bapak's passing.

In addition to answering questions to the best of their ability in the light of Bapak's advice and their own inner indications, helpers are also available, when appropriate, to 'test' with or for members as a means of helping them obtain clarity and direction in their daily lives. 'Testing' is a rather inexact translation of the practice of formulating specific questions and then seeking guidance via the latihan.

All we can bring to the latihan, advised Bapak, is an attitude of patience, sincerity and surrender to the will of God. Only God Himself can do the rest, which is nothing less than the initiation of a uniquely personal process of purification and spiritual development. This usually begins on the physical level, a stage many have associated with a general improvement in health, sometimes accompanied by specific and occasionally quite dramatic cures. The latihan gradually penetrates to the deepest aspects of one's being as the inner self is brought to life and grows to assume its rightful place.

When this true self comes into its own, it automatically creates a balance between our inner and outer lives, able to regulate and be served by the lesser forces that help to make up our nature rather than being ruled and often misled by them as before.

Such a process of purification and transformation calls for an increasingly complete and unconditional surrender to God if one is to remain truly sincere on the path of spiritual progress. If the cleansing action of the latihan is to be maintained, it may sometimes call for the correction of bad habits and inappropriate behaviour. We may even be called upon to let go of such ostensibly worthy objectives as the aspirations for perfection, justice and understanding, if these natural desires are wilful obstacles to our surrender.

Bapak's term for the passions and desires that arise from the lower aspect of our being and work through our hearts and minds was the *nafsu*. But, although it is convenient to speak of these ancillary forces – the material, vegetable, animal and ordinary human – as 'lower' and 'separate' Bapak said, the deeper reality is that everything merges in a total oneness. He also reminded us that these lesser levels of being, although sometimes seen as obstacles to spiritual growth, are actually essential for our existence in this world. "Man remains man," Bapak said, and the lower forces will always be part of our life in this world and should indeed be used for our benefit in this realm. It is not necessary or appropriate, he told us, to use our thinking mind to dwell upon the spiritual, or even to seek God. The mind and heart are our tools for making our way here on earth. Just as the tiger has his claws, so man has his thinking and intelligence.

On the worldly level, Bapak constantly urged us to "put the latihan into practice" by setting up business enterprises, both as an expression of individuality and self-reliance and as commercial ventures in which we could pool our expertise and learn to work together in harmony. He also encouraged us to identify and develop our true talent through following the latihan so that, ideally, the career we pursue, the work we do, would be in accordance with our own inner nature.

Through enterprises, said Bapak, we would learn to be guided by God in our everyday life exactly as in the latihan itself. Thus we would take care of our two main areas of responsibility: on the one hand to worship God, and on the other to provide for our needs in this world.

It was also Bapak's hope that the pursuit of enterprises would also enable the Subud association to contribute towards the creation of welfare projects for the benefit of the weak and needy in society at large "without distinction as to nation, social level or situation." Much is already being achieved in this direction in more than thirty countries under the auspices of

Susila Dharma International,[1] a Subud network officially affiliated to ECOSOC, the U.N's Economic and Social Council. In
most cases, these endeavours began as the fruit of an individual's
inspiration or inner guidance.

◆ ◆ ◆

Bapak sometimes compared the inner awakening set in motion
by the latihan to the opening and blossoming of a flower, a
process that progresses of itself and in its own season. He
warned against wishing to copy someone else, to be like anyone
else. "You will become *you* from head to toe," he said. "You will
be complete." He also explained that, because of the spiritual
connection from generation to generation, the action of the
latihan within us would also benefit, cleanse and lift up our for-
bears, suggestive of an inner reversal of the four Old Testament
references to 'the sins of the fathers being visited upon their
descendants.'

At the same time, the path of purification and growth can be
painful from time to time, especially as one is made all too
aware of one's own particular faults and failings, and when one
is required to let go of limited ideas of one's true identity. Not
that this process should be a matter of breast-beating and self-
condemnation. Bapak expressed it perfectly when he said,
"Mankind is required only to surrender, to surrender with acceptance and a willingness to let go." Awareness is all as the subtle process of separation between the inner feeling and the
forces with which we may have been identified, unfolds.

In extreme cases, this process may lead to a state of crisis, a period of especially intense purification when deep, fundamental
aspects of a person's nature are exposed and worked upon by
the *latihan*. The form such a manifestation takes will vary from
person to person and will reflect the individual's character. An
all-out spiritual crisis is relatively rare, and the likelihood of ex-

---

[1] http://www.susiladharma.org

periencing one may be lessened by adhering to Bapak's advice not to over-indulge in the latihan, not to try and 'go faster than God.' Nevertheless, he also said that although a crisis may be considered undesirable, someone who was obliged to undergo such an experience would afterwards be glad of it.

At this point, I should reiterate that although in my own case, the unusual experiences that make up much of the content of this book came about during an extreme crisis, they are not by any means a typical result of following the latihan.

♦ ♦ ♦

It is no more possible to adequately describe the latihan itself to anyone who has not had experience of it than it is to anticipate what any given man or woman will encounter in his or her own exercise. This will depend entirely on the nature of each individual and is an exclusively personal experience for everyone.

For each half-hour latihan the domination of the emotions and thinking is to an increasing degree reduced and set aside by the power of God, resulting in a state of clarity of heart and peace of mind that many people find carries over progressively into their outer lives. During the half-hour latihan each person gives free reign to whatever sound or movement may arise within them. As the process, and its developing awareness, progresses, one is trained more and more to move and act from the inner self. One thus becomes gradually accustomed to recognizing and feeling the difference between an inwardly guided state and one's 'normal' condition of moving and acting under the influence of what should more appropriately be our subordinate powers. It is through this awareness that the latihan begins to transform the way we approach our outer and otherwise ordinary lives.

An increasing awareness of this kind of spiritual chemistry is the essence of the latihan experience. It is the automatic outcome of each person's receiving – a term used, by the way, to describe both the content of the latihan itself as well as the inner guidance and indications that may manifest at other times.

At any one group latihan, different people might be laughing, crying, jumping, dancing, praying, chanting, singing, kneeling, or indeed being absolutely still and quiet. If this sounds bizarre, so must in their time have seemed the behaviour of David 'dancing before the Lord with all his might' (2 Samuel) and the Pentecostal fervour of the first disciples (Acts), together with the spontaneous movements of the early Quakers. As Bapak said, "It may seem strange, but it's real." I often think that the Coca Cola slogan - *It's the Real Thing* - may well have been coined with the latihan in mind!

Not that this contact with the Great Life Force is new, Bapak told us. It is in fact the foundation of the entire universe, the birthright of every creature, the source of all the religions and of Life itself. In addition to the major prophets, Bapak also cited George Fox and the 12th century Shaikh 'Abd al-Qadir al-Jilani as having received what we call the latihan.

Men and women exercise separately and, to begin with, members are advised to limit their latihan to two sessions a week with the local group. Later, when accustomed to the experience, they may feel it appropriate to add a third latihan alone at home. In addition, most people find that the occasional spontaneous latihan arises within them from time to time, an occurrence that becomes increasingly frequent as their growth progresses. In fact, Bapak would say that if we truly surrender to God we will be aware of the presence of the latihan state in the midst of *whatever* we do, a Subud equivalent of what many Christians would call 'prayer without ceasing.'

Bapak expressed this ideal beautifully in August 1986, less than a year before his death:

It is important to stay in touch with the latihan: to feel the vibration when you get up in the morning . . . to remember to feel for the vibration when you are in the middle of working . . . to bless your food at lunch, and allow the latihan to rinse out your activities. During the afternoon, feel the vibration once or twice. At supper, bless your food and get quiet. Don't wait for Wednesday night or Sunday night to surrender. God has given you the chance to live near Him day by day; don't relegate Him to once or twice a week.

♦ ♦ ♦

All we can do from the outer point of view to aid the inner self in its journey of liberation and purification, counselled Bapak, is to practice a form of self-denial (prihatin) whenever it may feel necessary. This can take the form of occasional fasting – on Mondays for outer needs and goals, for example, and on Thursdays for such aspects of the spiritual as nourishing inner patience and quiet – or cutting back on sleep or on other habits and pleasures.

Bapak also attached great importance to observing the annual month-long fast, whether the Lent of Christianity or the Ramadan of Islam. These are actually identical in essence, value and intent, he said, and represent the only thing a human being can actively do to 'help' Almighty God. He went so far as to say that, health permitting, the yearly fast is essential for anyone who is serious about the spiritual life.

For many in both East and West, the keeping of this holy month of fasting could be said to have degenerated into something of an empty ritual, limited perhaps to the equivalent of giving up chocolate for Lent. But, Bapak explained, if done properly, the weakening effect often implicit in the *outer* observances of the full fast should in fact serve to facilitate the *true* fast, namely, the *inner* abstinence from unworthy thoughts, desires and actions.

It may well seem strange that so many non-Muslim Subud people are in the habit of keeping Ramadan. For many, this is undoubtedly because it felt especially significant to be able to fast at the same time as Bapak himself for so many years. But it may also be that Ramadan is perceived as offering a more structured, well-defined programme than the rather vague, diluted Western approach to Lent. (A friend and Subud brother who for a while was a full member of a monastic order was actually forbidden to fast for Lent!) Each annual fast becomes a process in its own right, not unlike the latihan itself. It is again unique to each person, an act of willingness rather than an act of will.

◆ ◆ ◆

Once the contact has been transmitted from one person to another, the latihan arises freely and spontaneously and is received in full consciousness. It cannot be compared to meditation or to methods of visualisation or concentration upon mantras and the like. Neither is it a teaching, since all the teaching humanity needs has already been given by the founders of the great religions. In connecting us to the teacher within, the 'inner guru' that is our true identity, it has the power to restore life and understanding to religion. Many Subud members of widely diverse beliefs can bear witness to the truth of these words, testifying that the latihan has brought them back to their own religion, their faith clarified and strengthened.

With the latihan, Bapak explained, God involves Himself *directly* in the affairs of all those who receive it, making His power and guidance freely available to ordinary men and women who sincerely wish for this contact in the midst of their everyday lives.

Through following the latihan with complete patience, surrender and sincerity, we have the hope of reaching the level of a true human being and of attaining to the noble qualities symbolised by the words *Susila, Budhi* and *Dharma* – a process of development and growth that, begun in this world, can continue in the life after death.

This is possible because the latihan reconnects us with the inner self with which we were united while in the womb, but which we gradually forgot as we became increasingly identified with the forces of this world interacting through the heart and mind.

So this latihan, which seems strange and new, is actually very old. "This latihan" said Bapak, "is exactly the same as was received by all the prophets and the messengers of God in the past: by the Prophet Abraham, by the Prophet Moses, by Jesus Christ, by the Prophet Muhammad."

Bapak's words are validated by the fact that Subud groups include members from every major Faith, all doing latihan together without any of the deep divisions that might be expected in such get-togethers. Nowhere is this affirmation of the intrinsic oneness of the human race more in evidence than at a Subud world congress. At these gatherings, people of all creeds and colours and from all walks of life find themselves united – enveloped and guided by the great grace of the latihan.

Such a spontaneous fusion of rich and poor, of Muslim, Jew, Christian, Buddhist and Hindu, as well as of those who would profess no particular religion, demonstrates that a direct unifying contact with the Divine source is now available to all people everywhere, so that – as Bapak put it – we will not discriminate against one another, but, on the contrary, we will respect each other, help each other and love each other.

Glossary

Bapak: Indonesian word for father or respected older man. In this book it refers to Muhammad Subuh Sumohadiwidjojo, also known as Pak Subuh.

Contact: The receiving of the latihan, also known as the *Opening.*

Helper: An experienced Subud member who has been authorized to pass on the contact to others of the same sex.

Latihan kejiwaan: Indonesian words meaning spiritual exercise. Usually abbreviated to latihan.

Receiving: The guidance and experiences that arise within oneself when doing the latihan.

Rohani: The fifth level of being: that of the perfect human, completely surrendered to the Will of God.

Nafsu: The passions that animate the feeling and thinking.

Subud: An abbreviation of three Sanskrit words, Susila Budhi and Dharma, encompassing the meaning of all three of those words:

> **Susila:** Right living in accordance with the Will of God.
> **Budhi:**   The divine power residing within man.
> **Dharma:** Submission with patience, trust and sincerity to the Will of God.

Subuh: Indonesian word meaning dawn and having no direct connection with the word *Subud.* Bapak was given this name because he was born at dawn.

QUICK ORDER FORM

U.K. orders:
Simply mail this form to Dawn Chorus Publishing,
P.O. Box 2184, Gloucester, GL3 9AU

Please send me a copy of 'The Dawning.'
I enclose my cheque for £11.50 (being £9.95 + £1.55 p&p)

Name _____

Address _____

_____

Overseas orders:
Please email dawncp@blueyonder.co.uk for pricing and PayPal details.

QUICK ORDER FORM

U.K. orders:
Simply mail this form to Dawn Chorus Publishing,
P.O. Box 2184, Gloucester, GL3 9AU

Please send me a copy of 'The Dawning.'
I enclose my cheque for £11.50 (being £9.95 + £1.55 p&p)

Name _____

Address _____

_____

Overseas orders:
Please email dawncp@blueyonder.co.uk for pricing and PayPal details.

QUICK ORDER FORM

U.K. orders:
Simply mail this form to Dawn Chorus Publishing,
P.O. Box 2184, Gloucester, GL3 9AU

Please send me a copy of 'The Dawning.'
I enclose my cheque for £11.50 (being £9.95 + £1.55 p&p)

Name _____

Address _____

_____

Overseas orders:
Please email dawncp@blueyonder.co.uk for pricing and PayPal details.